Fear Less
vs
Fearless

♡

The Journey of a Lifetime

Malia Miles Lane

FROM MALIA'S MILES BLOG
Readers are saying

Malia Lane, I have been following you for a couple of years now. You inspired me to change my life. I bought an RV over the Thanksgiving holidays. I am on my 4th day of retirement - weird. I will be full-timing RV living as of January 31. I took this big step because of reading about your journey. I live in Austin and I am sending you love and peace. Thank you for continuing to share about your life. *Carol W.*

Malia, you were one of the first ladies of RV travel that I found on the internet. I'm still not able to start my journey but hope to do so in the next couple of years. Thank you so much for being there and inspiring all of us to change our lives for the better, to not fear doing it, and enjoying the journey as well. *Natalie A.*

Malia Lane, I hope you know how much your journey has inspired me to keep on keeping on. When I had the stroke they thought that was the end of me. Moments when I felt like it was too hard, I thought of you and your journey. We are all stronger because of each other. Love you and your spirit. *Diana H.*

The impact you've had on so many people in such a short time (really) is so incredible! "Well done my good and faithful servant" is what comes to mind. What a mark you have made on this earth and in ways you probably never dreamed of. The friendships you've forged and the lives you've touched in countless ways is beautiful. Thank you for being You in all your transparency and for all the valuable lessons you've shared along this journey called life. *Pamela V.*

I love how you're sharing your life with us. I have been following you for a couple of years now. You inspired me then, but mostly after losing my husband. You, as a solo full time RVer, give me hope and inspiration. I look forward to that day. *Barbara M.*

DEDICATION

To Don Emerson, my chief 'earth angel,' for being my mentor and best friend. Your confidence in me, even when I lacked it in myself, is what helped make my entire journey a more positive experience.

To my daughter, Angelique, who never gave up on the teenage mother who had a lot of growing up to do alongside her. You've been such a gift to me and your unfailing love and understanding has meant the world to me.

To my daughter, Keala, who also faced too many challenges being raised by a mother who still had no clue what she was doing half the time. Thank you for hanging in there with me as best you could.

To my granddaughters Caitlin and Anna, my great-granddaughters, Cailie and Cadence, for never making me feel guilty for the time away from them while chasing my travel dreams. My times with you whenever I landed back home were always the most precious.

My amazing niece, Heather, helped me stay focused and on track with regular pep talks, giving me practical tips and the encouragement to press on. Thanks, coach!

Thanks to my brother, Johnny, and sister-in-heart, Lois for always being there for me throughout all these years even when they don't agree with me all the time.

To the angels in the spiritual realm that have been my constant companions on this journey as well as the many other earth angels along the way that have had my back. To the people and spirit of Sedona, those magical beings I met there such as my precious friend, Nema, who insisted I would be guided through this process. She was right!

My cup runneth over.

CONTENTS

Where there is fear, there is a master.
Either you will master fear or fear will master you.
But there will be a master.
- Blackwolf Jones

PROLOGUE

In early 2001, I attended a three-day *Conversations with God* retreat with author Neale Donald Walsch, held in Sedona, Arizona. I was at a crossroads in my life, mainly relating to my work. I'd never had a job I truly liked and was always envious of those who could make money while enjoying what they did. Although my work as a legal assistant paid reasonably well (especially since I have no college degree), it wasn't personally fulfilling in any way. That retreat was the push I needed to live the life I truly wanted.

During the retreat, we were asked a million-dollar question that ended up changing my life, "What would you do if you had no fear?"

My instant reaction was that I was going to fail this course because I couldn't even imagine what it would be like to have no fear. I was full of it - taking action vs. not taking action - no matter the idea, I could find a fear to fit and talk me out of it.

Even though I couldn't form an answer in my head, my heart knew the answer was 'travel,' but going across country seemed as impossible to me as traveling to the moon. I wanted to see the beautiful scenery and national parks - but I hate air travel and hotels, so that makes that particular dream a bit of a problem.

But he wouldn't let us off the hook with excuses and insisted we answer the question. With the attitude of a petulant child being forced to participate against my will, I answered that I would travel. That wasn't a new dream, but so what? It felt like the impossible dream for someone like me. I certainly didn't have any extra money after paying rent and bills. And actually, I hated all the logistics of the travel process: going through airports, flight delays, baggage claims and staying in strange hotel rooms was never my idea of a fun time. In addition, having only two weeks of vacation a year was just not enough for what I envisioned as the real rewards of travel.

Too many of us are not living
our dreams because we
are living our fears.

- Les Brown

Sometime after attending the retreat, I eventually began having my own "Conversations with God."

These conversations usually started out as prayers asking for what I thought I needed or desperately wanted. Although I would ask God to direct and give me guidance, I also always tried to insert my own bright ideas about how it could be done: means, methods and timelines that I thought would best suit me. So even then, total faith wasn't my greatest strength.

As a result of these prayers or conversations, I sometimes received what I call a download - where a big concept is just dropped into me all at once and I totally and instantly understand it, even though I can't justify it with words. It takes longer to say just a few words than it takes to understand the answer, so I can't explain it any better than that. I picture it as a discernible difference and instant access of information, even though it's not like all the dots are connected and every question answered at that point. And even when it seems clear what my next step should be, it's still easy to get discouraged, not to mention distracted.

While I was arguing what I thought were perfectly good reasons why I couldn't do what my heart wanted to do, I got one of those downloads that said, "Just get a house on wheels and work as you go." Strangely enough, I knew instantly what that meant.

When I made the decision to go for it and trade the security I thought I needed for the freedom I craved, here's how I learned that you don't have to be fearless to take those baby steps toward your dream. I share it in the hope that it will be of benefit to you as well.

*The journey of a thousand miles
begins with a single step.*

- Lao Tzu

*And despite it all, I'm still willing
to trade security for adventure.*

- Malia Lane

Part 1

Changing My Life

Many of our fears are tissue paper-thin,
and a single courageous step
would carry us clear through them.

- Brendan Francis

Chapter 1
BARGAINING WITH GOD
How I Began to Fear Less

Upon leaving the retreat in Sedona, I was totally excited and confident that I had been given the answer to making my dreams come true. But cold and harsh reality started to set in once I got home. When I began to study the logistics of everything involved in making it happen, I got a serious case of disbelief that I could pull off something that complex. *A house on wheels? Seriously?* I'd never driven anything larger than a van before and that was scary enough.

Normally, I am not a big meditator since my mind won't shut up for long, but I was trying to get some Divine guidance. The confidence level I had felt previously that I could do this turned into feeling clueless. So, in a combination of prayer, meditation and begging, I asked for some Divine advice. And what I heard quite clearly in my head - but outside of my head, if you know what I mean - was 'Fearless.' I actually snorted at that and thought, "If that's you, God, you're wasting your breath because you know damn well I'm not fearless!" (Yes, God and I are on swearing terms and He is used to it from me by now.)

Again, I clearly heard in a loving, fatherly and slightly amused tone, "I didn't say Fearless - I said *Fear Less.*" Whoa - in another major download, I understood what a big difference that little blank space makes! I got this huge concept, all in the blink of an eye. I didn't have to be completely fearless all at once. I just had to fear less - even if just a little less at a time - and I could still proceed. I didn't have to leap off the mountain in one move screaming "I AM FEARLESS," as I fell. When fear fell in my path, I didn't have to be tall enough to jump over it, but I could pause long enough to think about what was really happening and then figure out a way around

7

either side or even underneath the fear. I knew that despite how crazy it sounded, that if I just kept my eye on the prize and took baby steps toward it consistently, that I would succeed.

Baby Steps:

All I had to add and remember was that even baby steps count. And that very first step may be a doozy, but all the ones that are ahead, especially after a stumble, make the biggest difference.

I *heard* that this dream of mine would actually come true. I was told that I would not be alone and that miracles and angels (both the spirit and the earthly human type) would follow me wherever I went. I was also made to understand that I also had a job in this quest - that I was to BE *Inspiration* - that I was to help and inspire other people (particularly insecure women with fears of being alone) to be this special brand of crazy too.

However, the understanding of that brought up even more insecurities: How can I claim an identity as Inspiration when I am less inspired by myself than anyone else?

Once again, baby steps, even toward a better image of myself. I was perfectly willing to give God my ideas on how to make all this work. Isn't it about time I won the lottery? I think that is a rip-roaring idea, don't you, God? I think I amused Him once again as I then heard, "Now just how inspiring would that be to others? Everyone would be able to say, 'Sure, she could do it, she won the lottery. Give me that break and I can do it, too!'"

OK, OK, I get it - I don't particularly like it, but I get it. I understood that if I really wanted to be a blessing and inspiration to those I meet, I can't play small and it was time to step up and play in the big leagues despite my misgivings.

That was in February 2001 and even with recurring fear and doubts, I just kept repeating the mantra, "baby steps."

Miraculously, just four months later in June, I had bought my motorhome, rented my house and hit the road.

Then there was my mom:

One of the most unexpected miracles was the revelation my mom came to. Her first reaction to me taking off in a motorhome across the country was not the least bit positive. She saw it as absolutely crazy and irresponsible, not to mention what it would do to her life since we lived next door to each other; she believed she needed me to be there. Needless to say, there was dissension and tension between us. My mind goes back in time to the look of sheer disgust on her face with what felt like hatred dripping from her words, "You've done some stupid things in your life, little girl, but this is the stupidest!" Gone was the progress we had made at that point in our relationship from my rebellious teenage years; her words hurt but didn't surprise me. But they also didn't change my mind.

I was reminded of a time as a little girl when I was walking down the street holding my mom's hand. We passed a travel agency with posters of Hawaii in the window. I stopped and looked up at her and said, "Oh, mama, can we go there?" The look on her face was so incredulous that the message was loud and clear, 'Poor people like us don't get to go places like that.' I had bought into that fear for the longest time and if I didn't let go of that limiting belief about myself now, when would I?

I loved my mom and told her I was willing to do whatever I could to help her. I offered to help her move back to New Orleans since I wasn't going to live in Austin anymore. I would assist her in any way I could, but she wasn't going to guilt me into giving up my dream. I was going to become a full-time RVer no matter how crazy it sounded to anyone else.

It completely shocked me that after a couple of days, she came over and said, "I know you might think this is crazy, but God talked to me last night. He told me you are on a mission and I was to help you. I don't think it is crazy anymore and I will do all I can to help you. Do you want me to get boxes to help you pack? I'll go get the best ones from the liquor store - they're strongest."

Since I had not, at that point, shared with her all the details about my own conversation with God, this completely blew my mind. It also gave me further validation that I was on the right path - no matter what anyone else had to say.

Mom then became my biggest supporter, especially after I took her on a few trips with me to places she had always dreamed of going. Those trips created a bond between us and strengthened our relationship in ways that I still cherish to this day. I will share some of those times in a later chapter because I learned so much from them.

My hippie youth put me at odds with most of my family while I was growing up and I was just rebellious enough at that time not to care. But the fact is we all crave acceptance, or at least to be understood and our perspective respected, especially from those we love.

Lessons Learned: There is a particularly sharp pain that comes from feeling rejected by your family, by those closest to us, or being told by them that your dreams are crazy and impossible. It feels like a personal attack on your abilities and their judgments have the power to hurt the most. They know us, which is why their opinions hold the most weight. What if they're right and we can't make it? Whether you want to hear them or not, their voices are the loudest. However, it is your life to live, mistakes and all. What if you really can succeed despite not one other person believing you can? You'll never know until you try. In the words of Lucy Spraggan, *"I know what you're scared of. I can feel it too. You're not scared of climbing mountains. You're scared you can't make them move."*

Chapter 2
WHAT WILL PEOPLE THINK?

People often say they couldn't imagine not having a stable home and what would they do with all their *stuff*? It was certainly an interesting process going through all the possessions I had spent my life accumulating to see what was really important to me and what could be let go. I was able to cull through it all and save everything I wanted into a 10x10 storage building I had built in the backyard of my side of the duplex that mom and I owned. I rented my side out and that even resulted in a profit between what the rent was and the mortgage payment. Besides all my stained-glass supplies (my favorite hobby) and a few pieces of furniture that I just loved, I filled that building to the brim with boxes of things I just didn't think I could part with. When I went through it for the first time in 10 years, I was thinking why had I kept half that crap?

So, in my RV, I still have stuff, and it's not like I don't have a home - I just have one whose backyard changes all the time...sometimes it's a forest in a state park, sometimes a lake, sometimes an ocean, sometimes a Wal-Mart parking lot. But I still have everything I need with me all the time - my own bed, my own bathroom, my own kitchen and best of all, all my clothes - I never have to worry if I have forgotten to pack something. Most importantly, for the first time in a long time, I could honestly say I loved my life and looked forward to every day.

Many people (especially women) say they'd love to do what I do, but they're too afraid. I tell them it's not like I don't have fear and insecurity. I firmly believe it's possible to move past them and live your life so you don't have regrets when you're too old to do anything else but sit in a rocking chair reliving your memories. Create lots of memories now so you won't be so bored then!

My Dream:

I always hope to touch everyone I meet along this journey in a positive way - to be an instrument and demonstration of all that is possible for every one of us. If nothing else, I can demonstrate that if I can do something so seemingly improbable, then so can anyone else.

To this day, when people hear that I am a full-time RVer, they often ask what first gave me the idea to do something so 'crazy.' Many say that travel is a secret desire of theirs, but they'd never have the guts to actually do it. I can relate to that. For years, I told myself I didn't have enough of some things and too much of others. I didn't have enough money, courage or time to pursue my dreams - and I had too many responsibilities and too much fear. The short answer to what finally pushed me out the door is that I once read of a study done with people near the end of their lives. They said that in review, their regrets were for all the things they hadn't done, not so much for what they did.

Armed with that belief, when I was honest with myself about what I really wanted, I knew it was to travel around the country, even if I couldn't begin to comprehend how I could pull that off. At the retreat, when I heard the answer to those concerns as, "Get a house on wheels and work as you go," I understood instantly what that meant. Even though I had never heard of the full-time RVing lifestyle before, my best friend, Don, had bought an Airstream and started traveling the country after his divorce the year before. The pictures he shared, especially of magical Mount Rainier, had me totally jealous. But it had not occurred to me that I could do something like that.

Having been raised in a poor family, I grew up operating in a mindset of lack, never having enough of whatever it took to do what I wanted. Therefore, I thought I was doing okay just to be able to pay rent and support my kids. Now that I was 50 years old, thoughts of my health possibly fading convinced me it was time to do the kind of exploring I always wanted to do and I should start doing it now. If not now, when?

Oddly enough, I somehow knew I could support myself no matter where I was, even if I couldn't explain it in a way that made sense to more practical-minded folks.

I also encountered some who would say what a wonderful idea it was, but you could see in their eyes the judgment of my dream failing. I learned to stay away from those robbers of my peace and got over feeling like I had to justify myself or 'sell' my ideas to anyone else.

Lessons Learned: There is never a shortage of discouraging naysayers. There will always be those who are willing to crap on your dreams. No matter if they say it's for your own good and they're trying to protect you; just don't buy into their fear! It's your life and you have the right to it, mistakes and all.

I think we all tend to judge ourselves more harshly than anyone else would and we tend to think ourselves less capable than we really are. But even if we only take baby steps away from those notions, we are perfectly capable of making even our wildest dreams come true.

Chapter 3
EARTH ANGELS
People Who Help

Thankfully, for all the discouragers and those secretly or overtly wanting you to fail, there are plenty on the other side to offset them.

The first earth angel who helped me along in this quest was my best friend and greatest inspiration, Don. When he bought an Airstream and started touring the country, we continued to communicate by email and I grew jealous of his travels. But at the time, it never crossed my mind that I could do anything like that.

He was an integral part of making all of my dreams possible and I've always considered it my greatest blessing that he traveled alongside me when I was first getting my dream off the ground. Don in his Airstream and me in my motorhome, we would chat with each other over the CB during travel time; it was such fun sitting around campfires at night. He knew all the star constellations and introduced me to them, with stories of who they portrayed. Having someone experienced (and so patient) like him to show me the RVing ropes and help untangle them was invaluable.

His generous spirit and hilarious sense of humor made my journey more enjoyable than I even imagined it could be. He was also one of the best teachers I have ever had. When I was concerned that my travel style was too pokey and I was taking too long getting to Seattle, I asked if he wanted to get there sooner. His reply was, "Where I want to be is wherever I am." I still crave that kind of contentment with what is, instead of what I think I want. *Be Here Now* was a book by Ram Dass I read early on but still hadn't mastered that concept.

14

So, I tried to follow his example and once I searched my heart, found my faith and made up my mind, things then fell into place at an incredible rate. When hearing of my plans, people seemingly dropped from the heavens to help me. They kept using the word 'inspiration' to describe their reaction to what I was doing and they wanted to help, even if it was just encouraging me to follow my dream. That is why that word became so important to me and why I chose '*Inspiration*' as the name for my rolling home.

Finding my Perfect RV:

Other indispensable angels who appeared were the people who sold me my RV home. There is not a doubt in my mind that this was a serious case of kismet that got us together. I had been working with Rob Hoffman, an RV dealer salesman who had been great about educating me about the many different choices I had. I had been looking at little 24-foot Class C models and wondered how in the world I would drive something that big, but at the same time, it felt too small to live in full-time. I had come to trust Rob, and as he learned my vision for my life on the road, he steered me in the larger Class A motorhome direction. At first, I wouldn't even go inside one of those huge beasts because I didn't feel there was any way I could drive anything like that! He then told me about a couple he had sold a motorhome to just last year and now they couldn't travel and had to sell. He offered to introduce us to each other and see if we could be the perfect match. Not working through a dealer meant there would be a savings without those extra costs and sales fees, so I decided to at least go look at it.

The first time I walked in and saw that humongous windshield, I knew that's what I wanted to look out of as I motored down the road. I joked that I was buying the windshield and would have to learn how to drive the rest of it! It was only a year old and a top of the line Winnebago motorhome. When I heard the asking price, I quickly regretted even going to look at it; no way could I afford

15

anything like that, no matter how good a deal it was, I reasoned.

The fact that it finally worked out was another case of divine providence. How unlikely to find an RV salesman who cared more about his customers than his commission - and a retired couple who cared more about who was buying their 'baby' than their profit, because they knew how much I would appreciate it. They became dear friends and were thrilled to have a part in my journey. I vowed to carry on the gifts they extended to me by paying it forward and continuing the circle of generosity every chance I got.

Learning to Accept Gifts:

One of the things I had to learn early on in the journey was how to accept gifts. Whether it's a personality defect or what, I find it hard to ask for or accept help. I say I want to do things and then when people offer to help me achieve my goals, I don't want to accept it - like that's a sign of weakness. I want to do it all myself and if I can't go it alone, I tend not to do it. If I had stuck to that position, I'd still be stuck in Austin.

Like Don told me when I balked at accepting all the help he so graciously offered, "You tell me all the time that I am your angel - so when an angel gives you a gift, you don't refuse it." I've thought a lot about that and I've come to realize that I can't pray for my dreams to come true and then refuse them if they don't come in a package wrapped just precisely the way I want or expect them. That's like putting an ad in the paper and then taking your phone off the hook. People are calling to answer your request but you're just not hearing them; that is wasted effort if nothing else. The dream is what is important. If I am given miracles and angels and gifts along the way, I should be thankful and accept and keep the movement of such gifts flowing without jamming up the works with resistance. I will be the one on the other end of the giving circle at some point and I would want my gifts to be received as happily and freely as I want to give them.

16

I've always been easily moved to tears when hearing tales of the kindness of strangers - truly selfless acts and seemingly small testimonies to the human spirit that show us who we really are in our heart of hearts. These are the people who make up for those who can't be bothered unless there's something in it for them. These are the people who teach us that despite the indifference and even downright evil of some - that there is truly more of the good than bad in the world. They show by shining example that like the smallest candle brightens the darkest room, that light is always more powerful than darkness.

I have had countless encounters with these kind of earth angels. I never feel like I can properly thank them, but I will never forget them. I wonder how many times people have touched our lives that never know of the impact they have and the difference they can make with a simple gesture.

Here is another validation I received: Tony ('Firedude') is a retired fire captain with a resultant painful lingering injury following many heroic rescues, but he defied the odds and followed his dream of becoming a full-time RVer. I responded to one of his posted musings about not wanting to get caught at the end of life full of regrets instead of full of memories of dreams fulfilled. I said what he had written had really inspired me and that I never used that word lightly. I got a return email saying he was bowled over when he went to my website after reading my post because it was ME that helped inspire him to begin full-time RVing! He wrote:

> *Even before starting my 'dream' I had discovered your link and had read much of your journal and followed your writings. And I am still amazed… you were one of my main catalysts before beginning and living my dream. You speak of the inspiration I gave you and here you were the one who sparked my dream and told me to live it.*

I tell you, this life has given me many blessings in many ways, but it's the interaction with people like this that is one of my greatest joys.

17

My First Speaking Engagement:

Tab, one of my best cyber-buddies, a fellow Escapee, began organizing the Graduating Full-timing Class of 2005. At that time, it was a group of about 65 couples and a few singles who were starting their full-time RVing lifestyle sometime in 2005. They all intended to meet at the big RV rally in Quartzite in January 2006.

Tab first wrote me in 2004, "I wish I could fully express how much you have an influence on our journey with your fearless adventure to overcome things and do it by yourself. Thank you from the bottom of my heart! I eagerly await each update you send; your trip to Yellowstone immediately prompted us to make it a must see. Your pictures are so beautiful and you certainly have a way of writing that captures the attention. You never cease to amaze me."

When he first asked where I would be next January and asked if I'd come to Quartzsite to speak to the group, I laughed and said I didn't become a full-time RVer to plan that far ahead. The more I thought about it though and the more I read from the Class, I thought of it as an honor to be asked, so I happily agreed. I'm sure people like Tab, whom I've never met, but who have 'met' me through my journals, don't realize how much it means to me to hear from them. They have no idea how much encouragement I get from their taking the time to let me know I have impacted their lives positively in some way.

He said he thought everyone would want to hear about my trip through Alaska, as it seems that is the Mecca destination for all RVers. I told him I'd probably be more nervous about speaking before the group than I was in the 'wilds' of the tundra, but I'd tell them anything they wanted to know. And it turned out that the warm welcome they gave me made me feel like a star!

Rich in Blessings:

There have been times I've been invited over for fantastic dinners or out for fun excursions at such perfect timing to get me out of whatever doldrums I was going through at the time. I've been encouraged to continue my journey even when I get scared and discouraged by relative strangers who somehow were guided to know and say just what I needed to hear at the perfect time.

I've been blessed with people responding to my thanks by thanking me for letting them help me. "We just happened to be in the right place at your wrong time to help out. Thanks for letting us be part of the solution."

Whenever needed, I have been reminded by others who recognize my struggles because they've had the same issues, that I need to just continue pressing onward and count my blessings instead of what seems like the occasional curses.

Lessons Learned: It is rather rare that we have both the opportunity and the means at the same time to help out a fellow being. Whenever I am in that position and have made a difference to someone, it always makes me feel so good inside, I almost feel selfish - like I got more benefit than the person who supposedly needed the help. I hope to also remember that we're all in this together and I shouldn't deprive others of the same experience by not letting them help me.

Chapter 4
DOES SIZE MATTER?

As I was writing about the process of getting my first motorhome and the earth angels involved, this seems a good place to share a related article I wrote for RVTravel.com, published on February 20, 2013:

Fear of the Big Rig:

It bugs me a bit to hear other women say they couldn't do what I do - no way could they drive a giant motorhome around the country, especially towing a car. It's not that I can't relate to their fear, but I can also testify that they really can do what I do if they really want to. Feeling fear doesn't automatically require a full stop.

I remember how tiny I felt standing beside motor homes when I was looking for my RV home. I refused to even go inside of a Class A. For the first month I was looking at 24-foot class C's and wondering how I'd ever drive something that big -- I was intimidated driving vans, for goodness sake! But the first time some sneaky salesman got me inside a 36-foot Class A, I was hooked -- mainly by the humongous windshield that lets me see the sights from a broader perspective than from a truck viewpoint.

Once I decided I wanted one, then came getting it and harder yet, learning to drive it. I swear, it struck me as almost criminal that they'd give someone as inexperienced as me a license to drive something this big on public streets with no proof at all of my ability other than driving a little car. Really, shouldn't there be something more required than just dire warnings of "remember the wide turning radius rule?" Oh, yeah and don't forget, you can't stop as fast as you're used to. But as scared as I was at first, and even though I warned my neighbors on all sides to watch their mailboxes, I managed to get in and out of my driveway without hitting any. I'd have never guessed then I could become a confident big-rig momma.

An RV salesman I came to trust during my hunt told me the reason most people (especially those going full-time) trade in their RVs is because they bought too small initially. Usually you'll take more of a financial hit by trading up quickly than you would have by buying bigger to begin with. He also said the other really important thing is a slide - that little extra room makes a huge difference when you're parked and that motorhomes without them don't do as well on resale. On the forums, some RVers say they just don't trust them and don't think they're worth it because of leaks, mechanical failure, too much weight, whatever. All I know is that in the four years I've been full-timing, I've never felt cramped except when I had to have the slides closed when camping alongside the road or in another temporary spot. In my opinion, those few feet of living space greatly increase the livability. I don't think I'd ever buy another RV without one and wouldn't mind even having yet another slide-out -- those dually living room ones I've seen are really cool.

When I was at the Seattle RV show, I asked a couple of salespeople how it's different selling RVs to single women vs. couples. Glenn said that even with couples, the woman is usually still the decision maker. He said of motor homes, "if you can get women behind the wheel, 90 percent of the selling is done." Debbie said she tells women, "Now's not the time to be wimpy about size, ladies." That's always good for a chuckle. "It's so empowering to handle something that big so well," she says. Besides that, the big diesels have much more power, handle better, have a tighter turn ratio, better suspension and gives a much quieter ride. Who can resist that whole 'Mr. Wonderful' package?

I firmly believe that the female navigators of their rigs should learn how to drive them. It's a safety issue, if nothing else. If something happens to the pilot, the co-pilot should be able to take over the wheel and get them both safely home.

On an RV forum recently, one woman was encouraging another on her upcoming 'maiden voyage.' Her words were true, but also made me laugh at the picture painted of her 'first' time.

> *It's scary the first time you drive these things. I had to keep telling myself that someone famous once said, 'It's okay to be scared, as long as you just go out and do it!' I must have said that to myself 20 times the first time. My mouth was dry and I had to chew gum to stop from chewing my lip to pieces. Others suck on a lollipop. I have this vision of roads full of gum smacking lollypop chewing old ladies driving their big rigs! More power to us!*

When I got my first motorhome, the previous owners drove it into my driveway so that I could pack it up and get ready to roll. I had test driven some motorhomes from dealerships, but they always drove it out of the lots and then let me have the wheel once we were on straight streets or arterial highways. So, when it was time for me to leave, I went into a bit of a panic when I realized I'd have to drive this humongous thing on my city street and actually make left turns! But I made it down that street and many others without a scratch. So, take the big wheel by the horns, ladies! It may not always be easy but believe me, it's worth the effort!

Lessons Learned: Don't compromise what you want because of limitations that probably aren't as bad as you make them out to be. Whether it's the size of the RV you drive or if you can tow a car behind it, you won't know until you try. Don't just assume you will fail. Break through the barriers and decide to go for what you want instead of settling for less for any reason.

Chapter 5

HAWAII
A Dream Come True

Going way back in time now, travel to Hawaii was my first 'impossible' dream that I made manifest - before I had even heard of the concept of RVing, full-time or not. Moving to Maui in 1987 was actually one of the most powerful experiences of my life. It was my ultimate dream at the time manifested, but still with many fears attached, so it seems to belong here. Hawaii started as a childhood dream and since I knew I couldn't afford to visit there as much as I yearned to, I just decided to move there and make it my home! Whatever works, right?

As I mentioned earlier, walking down the street as a little girl with my mom and seeing travel posters of Hawaii in a travel agents office gave me the dream, but I never really thought it could come true. That was one of the very first memories I can recall before kindergarten. Even though I don't remember the words my mother used, she made it quite clear that it was an impossible dream for poor folks like us. Thinking back, that may have been the beginning of my understanding and/or accepting it as fact that I could not have the things I wanted.

Sometime in 1985, my love at that time had taken me on a vacation to Maui and Kauai. I knew from the moment that I set foot off the plane in Maui that it was my heart's home. That island had everything I loved about planet earth: crystal clear waters, towering mountains, the scent of flowers everywhere and all with perfect weather year-round. In my heart, I knew the 'aloha Spirit' was what I wanted full-time.

From Journal - April 25, 1986 (the week before my 35th birthday):

I was reading over goals that I had written down in 1983; I find them especially interesting now. This was part of an exercise suggested in a book I was reading at the time having to do with career development. I was to write down goals I'd like to achieve within certain time periods, no matter how unreachable they seemed or how many obstacles were in the way, or how many excuses my mind could conjure up as to why I couldn't get there.

I started small with those things that I felt were more easily obtainable and by now I had achieved those. Some of lesser priority had been left by the wayside for various reasons. But the last one - the ultimate and final dream I wrote down - that's the one I'm going for now with all my heart.

I came to this conclusion only a few weeks ago, but now it seems like something that's been brewing all my life. For so long I've felt this urgency to find out what I really wanted to do for a living. My executive secretary skills may pay the bills fairly well, but nothing about it touches my soul or gives me joy. I wanted the kind of passion that made me look forward to getting up in the morning and chomping at the bit to get to work. I thought that if I believed in something with that much conviction, nothing could stand in my way. The practical side of me wanted that passion to be tied to my job simply because you spend more time working than anything else, so why not love what you do and get paid for it?

The only problem was, I had no idea what that might be. In trying to figure it out, I consulted career guidance counselors and answered their forms to see what my natural strengths were and they all pointed to pretty much what I was already doing. I'm highly organized and detail oriented, so what? That's not exactly exciting material to work with, so what was wrong with me? Why couldn't I even think of a dream in this regard to pursue? Am I just destined to live this mechanical, unfulfilling life forever?

One career guidance counselor even got a little frustrated with me since I could not come up with anything. He leaned back in his chair and said, "Well, if you can't think of a job you really want to do, expand your horizons. Think of it this way: you can work in a job you don't like in a place you don't like - or you can work in a job you don't like in a place you love. Is there somewhere other than Austin you'd like to live? Let go of all limitations your mind is arguing. If you could live in a place that gave you that kind of joy of life - that type of enthusiasm - well, then you could work at any job and still be happy.

That made sense to me, so I finally gave my imagination room to wander. When answering those career guidance evaluations before about what you enjoy doing, I'd basically answered this way: "When I was 16, I ran away from home. I've been on my own since and in the process of having kids, growing up and making a living to support us, in that order. That has not left any time to figure out anything else."

So, I tried letting go of figuring out all the mechanics and making it fit into the box labeled with what I thought was remotely possible. His next instruction was, "So sit back, relax, close your eyes and tell me where you are when you feel the best and most at peace - when you are the happiest to be alive."

Maui - my Heart Place:

The image that leapt to my mind immediately was Maui - how I felt my soul become so alive and like my true self there more than I ever had before. Immediately, the thought of moving to Maui seemed as impossible as a trip to the moon. Therefore, I began to consider someplace on the west coast that had similar features to Hawaii; I started to look into research on San Diego.

My love, who had taken me to Maui for that life changing visit, is an astrologer and after consulting my 'astrocartography' chart and looking at a global map, here's what he had to say:

25

Well, if you're that determined, why settle?" Running his finger along the map, he said, "Now, if you really want to go somewhere where you would feel at home and probably would be most successful in all areas, look at the Hawaiian Islands.

As my gaze wandered there and I heard what he said, an intense feeling come over me that made it abundantly clear that I could do just that. Not only was it possible - it felt like my destiny. He read what the chart said, "A good and vital place to seek residence. Also good for business, employment, self-expression and spirituality."

I had one of those strong 'natural knowing' moments and I could not only concede the possibility, but the assurance that I could pull that off - I could feel what it would be like to live and work in Hawaii - particularly Maui.

And what had I written on that goal sheet from three years ago? For 1987, I entered, "Buy a condo in Maui." That seemed so farfetched back then that I was still only thinking of it in terms of an investment property that would allow me to visit there - not actually living there. But it turns out, that's the year I have determined I will move to Maui. I have never felt so confident about something that sounds so flakey in my entire life!"

What a ridiculously daunting thought - to move to Maui! My first step was getting my daughters on board, who were 17 and 13 at the time. Their initial reaction was extremely positive, or I would have given up the idea at that moment. Months later, after all details were put into motion (selling my little secretarial business and most of my possessions) at a time when it would have been unthinkable to give up, they both decided that they would rather stay with their dad and friends in Austin. My first thought was that there was no way I could leave them, no matter how old or whatever the situation. Suffice it to say for now that once it became obvious that they wanted the chance to make their own choices as to where they lived, they were still fully supportive of me moving to Maui. I finally decided to give myself permission to do what my heart wanted and that I should give them the same opportunity.

During this time, as I prayed for a message, I opened the *Course in Miracles* here:

> *You who have played that you are lost to hope,*
> *abandoned by your Father,*
> *left alone in a fearful world made mad by sin and guilt;*
> *be happy now. That game is over.*
> *Now a quiet time has come,*
> *in which we put away the toys of guilt*
> *and lock our quaint and childish thoughts of sin forever*
> *from the pure and holy minds of Heaven's children*
> *and the Son of God.*

Making it Happen:

So how exactly do I go about moving to Maui? Remember - this was 1986 and the Internet had still not been heard of at that point, at least by me. All the research tools that it offers (that make this kind of thing so easy now), were not available then, but I still had the powerful tool of speech and writing.

Some of the steps I took that made it more real for me: I subscribed to the *Maui News*. I studied the employment ads and rental availability. I ran an ad about my desire to move there looking for tips from people who had done the same. From those replies came some friendships and lots of great information. I ordered everything I could from the Chamber of Commerce and always drooled over the *Aloha Magazine* pictures and the thought of actually calling that my home.

It became apparent that the costs of rent and the wages paid did not seem compatible. Sometimes I'd get anxious and insecure, but when I opened the *Course in Miracles* twice in two days looking for a message, this is what came up:

> *...anticipate with present confidence. We will be sure that everything*
> *we need is given us for our accomplishment of this today.*
> *We will rest from senseless planning - today we will receive instead of*
> *plan.*

27

When I'd get too overwhelmed by the endless details, I'd just put it all down and start imagining how wonderful it would be once I was a resident of Maui, no matter what it took to get there.

I even took a night clerk job at a hotel in Austin a few months before departure. I figured having some hotel experience might be of help, that way I wouldn't have only secretarial experience.

From Journal - July 20, 1986:

> *As I am sitting here contemplating living in Hawaii, thinking about what I'd be leaving behind, how foreign it all felt, I began to feel a bit insecure. The thought then came to me that life is not stagnant - it is constantly changing, evolving, flowing into different streams. And this is good and as it should be.*
>
> *Then I turned on the local PBS TV station and Tim Cook, the minister of the Unity Church here, was saying that he was leaving his charge as minister, not really knowing what he was going to do next. But he felt the need now to be a student, not a teacher at this point in his life. He spoke of how even though the life he'd built was what he'd thought he wanted and his security was here, that he felt no great fear of giving it all up. He recounted many instances in his life of how when he'd lost everything that he thought was so important, it became evident later that things were always working for his higher good. His security was now vested in God and his belief that God does care and provide for us even as the birds of heaven.*
>
> *He spoke of the 'Pearl of Great Price' that Jesus tells of in the Bible and how when a pearl merchant chanced upon this most magnificent pearl, that he'd sell all his other pearls, beautiful though they may be, to obtain the great pearl.*
>
> *Hawaii must be that great pearl for me. And I trust in God to lead me there and reveal the beauty and value in it. And I'm so thankful.*

I saw this insert in the *Maui News* later: "Accept the wise counsel of Emerson, who wrote, "Place yourself in the middle of the stream of power *and wisdom which animates all whom it floats and you will be impelled to truth, to right and to perfect contentment."* I accept.

So, I just started talking to everyone I could about it. And of course, I was frequently met with confused stares that said, "What in the world makes you want to move to Hawaii? That's crazy!"

I almost got some cards printed that simply said, "No. No. No…because I want to!" Inevitably, the questions would go like this:

> *Whaaat? You're moving to Maui! Do you know anyone there?*
>
> *No.*
>
> *Do you have a job lined up there?*
>
> *No.*
>
> *Do you have a place to live?*
>
> *No.*
>
> *Then why in the world would you do something so crazy without all that in place?*
>
> *Because I want to!*

If I ever needed proof, other than it being my heart's deepest desire, my dreams confirmed that it was the right move for me. In one particularly powerful dream, I was riding a bicycle down the street waving to everybody and shouting that I was happy to be in Hawaii. And I remember thinking in my head as I was waving to all these native people that I had heard Hawaiians really didn't like *haole* (white or non-native to Hawaii) people too much and that maybe they really wouldn't welcome me in real life. But in my dream, I could hear the thoughts of the people on the porch and they were saying, "Oh no, that doesn't mean you. You have a true Hawaiian heart. Welcome." I remember waking in a truly blissful state.

The Mechanics of Moving:

However, the mechanics of such a move were surely daunting. I sold everything I knew would be impractical or unnecessary for living on a balmy island. I kept a few winter clothes because I knew there were parts of Maui and the Big Island that were above 10,000 feet and I intended to see the sunrise over Haleakala, where temps could get to freezing. I left some things I didn't want to part with, but wouldn't need on Maui, packed in a friend's garage. I shipped my car there because it was paid off and still relatively new and would be less expensive than buying something else once there. I remember it cost more to ship the boxed belongings I had decided I couldn't part with, across the country by truck than it did to ship by cargo over the ocean.

Sheila, a former coworker, who was also a travel agent, got so excited helping me with my plans, that she decided to come with me! That was a total blessing since we shared the cost of a condo at the reduced rent she was able to get us as an agent for that first week.

Shortly, I began to think moving there during the height of tourist season was not the best idea I'd ever had. Many landlords raised the rent significantly during the winter high season and would not offer even six-month leases. I started looking at tiny rooms in private homes and even they were $350-$450 a month. That might sound reasonable now, but in 1987, I remember being shocked and knew I couldn't handle that for long. To top it all off, some of the ones I checked out would not be acceptable roommates from the weird vibes I got. Yes, there are junkies even in paradise! But I kept telling myself I belonged there and something would pop up for me somehow, even though the rental agents I talked to laughed and said to call back in April and rates in the newspaper ads were enough to give me a heart attack.

Meanwhile, Sheila and I were doing all the touristy things like whale watching tours, snorkeling at Molokini and getting up super early to get up to Haleakala for the spectacular sunrise.

My favorite was the 52-mile drive to Hana, a narrow road with 620 curves and hairpin turns, and 59 one-lane bridges. For those who might find that scary, just take it slow. It is truly worth it as it is one of the most wondrous drives and destinations in the world. Experiencing the sight and feel of walking on the black sand beaches of Waianapanapa State Park on the way there, was an incredible adventure.

The day after Sheila left I had to vacate the condo but still had no place to call home there. My friend Cheryl, who had also moved there from Austin and had been my pen pal, offered me their couch. I certainly didn't relish the idea of being a third wheel in their tiny bungalow, but at least I wouldn't have to sleep on the beach.

That night, I prayed, "Father, I believe you led me here and I can't believe you intended me to be homeless, so please can you put a rush on it?" I swear, that very moment, I got a phone call from an owner who had not returned any of my calls for days. It was a lady who shared her home with one other woman in Maui Meadows. She had one other room to rent for $600 a month and once I checked it out, I moved right in. I started looking for jobs right away and sometimes felt a bit discouraged, but whenever I had doubts, I'd just go sit by the ocean and they were washed away.

From my journal on January 23, 1987:

> *I arrived here two weeks ago today. Sometimes it feels like I've been here all my life and at other times, it is like I can't believe I finally made it. After I watched my first sunset on Maui, I wrote my mother to thank her for giving birth to me. I had never been happier to be alive! I wake up in the early morning, walk just outside my door and see the mountains still holding pink low-lying clouds and the ocean on the other side, sometimes with whales breaching, an amazing sight!*
>
> *There is an abundance of rainbows and sometimes I just have to pinch myself to make sure I'm not dreaming. The sunsets here look like a huge vibrant red/orange beach ball descending into the ocean - absolutely awe-inspiring. I love this glorious island*

and feel sometimes that God made it just for me, I am so
blessed. The mana (spiritual energy) here is phenomenal and
feeds my soul perfectly!

It Keeps Getting Better:

My first job was as a temp receptionist at Maui Island
Mortgage. The biggest thrill was just to be able to say Maui
every time I answered the phone, which reminded me with a
tingle that I really had made it. Everyone talks about the
horrific traffic on the road between Kihei to Kaanapali and
it's true. Usually it's because tourists are driving turtle neck
speed and not caring that there are residents trying to get to
work. But nothing about the drive really bothered me. I had
the green West Maui Mountains on one side, Haleakala in
view and sparkling blue water to gaze at, so I just left early
enough to enjoy the drive.

None of my worries about being able to get a decent enough
job to support myself turned out to be true. First of all, I have
a strong work ethic and always got to work on time and didn't
mess around with personal stuff while at work. That was
really valued by employers there who were mostly dealing
with people who operated on 'island time' - meaning they get
there when they get there sometime around any expected
timeframe.

My first permanent job was as Sales Secretary at the Maui
Marriott. I ended up renting an apartment from the Director
of Sales that was right on the water on the Kaanapali side
where I worked, which was much more convenient. I put a
futon on the covered lanai and slept out there, where I could
be lulled to sleep by the sound of the ocean. Within a couple
of years, I became part of the opening management team of
the Embassy Suites Resort as Director of Guest Services
when it opened on the island in late 1988.

Spiritual Connection:

I was part of the group who were taken to the Big Island for
team building before the hotel opened. For sunset one day,

they took us to the edge of Halema'uma'u crater where a hula halau (dance troupe) danced a tribute to the goddess of fire, Pele. Imagine sitting at the rim of a volcano (even though it wasn't active at the time) but being able to see the fresh lava tracks snaking their way to the ocean – we were actually watching new land being created! We were able to watch the steam rise from the vents, the scent of sulphur in the air and felt the warmth of the ground under our feet. Then we were able to feel the throbbing of the accompanying native drumming; we watched in awe the graceful movements of the dancers as they told tales of their ancestors with their hands and chants. It was one of the most magical times I have ever experienced on this earth and it made me feel I had stepped back in time, recognizing how special this event was.

As the sun set and darkness fell upon us, the torches were lit; I could not help but just sit there and cry like a baby; I couldn't even understand why. One of the teachers came and sat by me and just put her arms around me. I told her I couldn't explain why, but I was excited and at the same time, extremely emotional watching the ceremony. I just could not stop crying and there was joy, but also sadness involved in all these swirling emotions.

This teacher just looked intently at me and told me this was all because I had lived here in at least one past life. That's why I felt compelled to come here this time, but that in doing so, I also had some karma to work out. She said that I had not forgiven myself for feeling I had betrayed my people by being more attracted to haoli ways when they began taking over the islands. This hurt my heart so much! Because now my most fervent desire was to truly belong here; yet in my mind, I knew I never would again, not in that way.

This guilt and sadness also coincided with how I'd always felt about Native Americans. Even as a little girl, when I saw movies about cowboys and Indians, I always rooted for the Indians. I have always thought it an unconscionable blight on our nation's history, the way we treated those who were here long before 'civilization.' And I still feel the same way to this day, about them and the Hawaiians.

Strangely enough, one of the reasons I was excited about moving to Hawaii was to study the Hawaiians' ancient religious beliefs, including Huna. The word means 'secret' and was the name Max Freedom Long gave in his book, *Huna, Recovering the Ancient Magic*, describing his metaphysical theory of ancient kahunas' teaching that each person is composed of three beings: the subconscious *(unihipili)* likened to a child before the age of reasoning, the inner being that is emotional and intuitive; next is the conscious, reasoning person *(uhane)*, who is waking consciousness, rational; then the super-conscious, highest self *(aumakua)*, the connection with the Divine. In reading his book, so much of this made sense to me in ways that I just could not explain. I should note here that Max Freedom Long's conclusions are not reflected in the Hawaiian language nor any traditional Hawaiian beliefs. But they still made more sense to me than the Catholic beliefs I was raised with.

I especially resonated with the attitude of ancient Hawaiians toward the divine and prayer. Rather than bowing in supplication with head lowered and arms down to a god they felt was there to dictate their every move and to punish severely for infractions, their stance was upright, head high, arms outstretched to heaven, eyes open, speaking as if to a loving father rather than a judgmental dictator. The attitude taken in their prayer was, 'help me do what I am capable of doing' - not 'do this for me.' And 'help me to find my shortcomings so I may correct them' - rather than 'forgive me my failure and make everything alright again.' The Taro plant is a big part of the Native Hawaiian diet. When they pick it from the boggy fields, they pray, 'Forgive me for taking the taro and thank you for the sustenance' and then planted a replacement. They always accompany prayer with effort and responsibility. I just thought it was cool that they practiced crop management in a spiritual way.

Hawaiians did not view themselves as totally unworthy and sinful. Specific wrongdoing merited punishment, atonement and seeking forgiveness, not accusations and self-abased feelings of being a generally depraved and despicable person.

In 1830, a missionary complained, "We find so little of that feeling of sinfulness and unworthiness a correct knowledge of the human heart and a clear discovery of the character of God always produces." Their attitude was one of not only respect for their gods, but self-respect. To them, gods were ever present - guarding, guiding, warning, blessing, as well as punishing when deserved. Spirits inhabited and assumed the forms of plant and animal life, rocks and streams, the sky, fire, the winds, thunder and clouds. This struck me as one of those 'natural knowing' moments that I just knew was closer to the truth than I'd ever been taught.

I loved everything about living on Maui, including frequent trips to the other islands. I loved the music, the luaus and am happy to report the Aloha spirit was alive and well if you looked past all the tourism development. I lived there from January 1987 until mid 1991, when I found out my oldest daughter was pregnant with my first grandchild. The distance between Maui and Austin became too far at that point. I did think then that I'd probably return in the future. However, that was not to be. When my next dream of RV travel around the country became a goal, I had no real regrets and only gratitude that I was so blessed to have lived there as long as I had. Aloha 'oe forever!

Lessons Learned: Talk to people about your dream - don't keep it buried inside yourself. Of course, there will be some who will try to discourage you. But you never know who might know someone or something who can help you progress toward your dream in unimagined ways!

No matter if you think the whole world is against you and you're not even sure of all the steps (or flights) it will take to get there, there is nothing that can stop you once you believe in yourself and your own power.

Just say NO when others try to persuade you that you can't possibly pull off your dreams; feel free to simply answer, "because I want to" and let it go. You don't owe anyone any other explanation. Just remember – 'baby steps!'

Some lessons are harder than others:

To this day, I have some regrets about that decision, but there was no way to know the ramifications that were to come that haunt me even now. I would bet that we all, at some point, wish we could go back in time at critical periods of our lives and just hit 'reset' for the chance to do it over, make up for past mistakes and get it 'right' this time.

One problem with that is that we don't recognize them when we're experiencing them. It's a mixture of Catch 22 and not seeing the forest for the trees. On one level we all get exactly what we need, even if we don't recognize it. Whether we label it a blessing or a curse, we created it. Maybe for karmic purposes, maybe just as a learning experience, who knows? But just as necessity is the mother of invention, then mistakes are the necessity of learning. But even with those regrets, I still believe it was the right choice for me at the time and that's what I focused on here.

Part 2

On the Road

Chapter 6
SUPPORTING AND ENJOYING MY TRAVEL HABIT

Back to my big RVing dream now - when I was initially inspired with the idea of getting a house on wheels and to work as I traveled around the country, I figured the best way to do that would be to get temp legal secretary jobs. I planned to land in places I really wanted to explore, knowing I would have to stay for longer periods since I'd be stuck in an office for five days a week. But that would still leave me weekends to get out and do the things I wanted to do wherever I was.

Maine (July - September 2001)

Don wanted to see the lighthouses in Maine and Acadia National Park, so I was happy to agree to that as our first destination. A southern gal all my life, I had never been in 'Yankee' country and I was very excited about that. We decided to stay close to Portland, figuring I'd have a better chance of working with agencies to get temp legal secretary jobs at law firms in large cities. I started the process of registering at agencies, but even though testing showed my skills to be great, I wasn't getting called for jobs. At the next agency I applied to, after going through their process and being complimented on my skills and resume, I asked the staffing counselor why I wasn't getting jobs.

He looked at me and said he probably shouldn't tell me this, but that temp agencies really made most of their money from placing temporary people to permanent positions. And a lot of law firms looked at using temp people as a way to try them out to see how well they worked. I told him I had pictured being used for things like secretaries on vacation or maternity leave, but he still wasn't very encouraging about my prospects.

To my horror, I then broke down sobbing and even stuttered, "But, but, - you don't understand, that's my whole plan!" He was sympathetic, but the best he could offer was a suggestion that at the next agency, I leave out the part about only being in the area temporarily so they would think there was the possibility of placing me permanently. Since I believe that is bad karma, if nothing else, I didn't want to lie as a regular part of my inspirational trip; that just did not feel like the right option. Fear tells us that we can't afford to keep our integrity and that sometimes it's just necessary to lie. That's the biggest lie and the worst path we can follow.

It was certainly too late to turn back now, so I knew I quickly had to come up with Plan B. I decided to try some self-marketing. I made my own business cards with my picture next to the RV, put together a short introductory letter, attached my resume and hit the streets visiting some of the largest law firms in areas that looked good for walking around at lunch time. I would introduce myself to the receptionist, give her my packet and ask her to give it to the personnel department head. I would get the name of that person and say I would follow up the next day.

A lot of times I didn't even make it home before I would start getting calls from people who were intrigued. A lot of them didn't have assignments to offer, but they just wanted to hear more about what I was doing because it sounded crazy to them…but wonderful.

My First Job on the Road:

Those efforts did pay off and it wasn't long before I started a new (supposed to be two-week) temp assignment at Pierce Atwood, a prestigious downtown law firm in Portland, Maine. Located in the historic district, it was full of older beautiful buildings and monuments among the high rises. I loved to walk around and go shopping at L.L. Bean, which I had never heard of before, but soon became addicted to. People would stop at my desk and exclaim, "Oh, I've heard about you - you're the lady traveling around the country in a motorhome!"

I never had a problem finding a lunch partner because everybody wanted to hear all about it. That idea was a real novelty back then and it's interesting how much more popular it is now.

That first job on the road was certainly memorable in many ways. It was September 11, 2001 when shortly after arriving one morning, I heard that the first floor of our building was being evacuated because the police were searching for a man with a gun. As we went to the windows to look out, we then heard people down the hall saying that the Pentagon had just been bombed and that two towers of the World Trade Center were burning. Our country was under attack; at that point we didn't know by whom.

Watching from the window, we could see policemen with shields and guns drawn entering the building across the street from us. Everything then seemed to me to begin moving in slow motion. I wondered if our building would be next and it crossed my mind in a curious way that maybe this was the day I was to die - how ironic before I got to fully explore my dream.

We were hungry for news, but there were no TVs on the floor and it was really slow going getting on the Internet. When I saw some of the first pictures coming through, there was a part of me that thought it must be some kind of hoax - a *War of the Worlds* type of show. It seemed inconceivable that we were actually attacked on our homeland; watching the scenes over and over again on the news that night did nothing to alleviate the shock - the sheer astonishment that this could really be happening and that so many people were undoubtedly dead.

I then got a call from one of my co-workers making sure I was OK and asking if I needed anything. As the new kid on that block, that really impressed me. When they found out I needed a ride home on Friday since Don was going to visit his daughter, they actually argued about who would have the privilege, which I found funny and touching at the same time.

From my journal shortly after the horrific day of 9/11:

I've never met a nicer group of people than those I am now blessed to work with. When they found out I needed a ride home on Friday and possibly to and from work on Monday, they actually argued over who would get to do it. It was kind of funny. There were emails back and forth at first deciding who was closest to where I am and who had the same work schedule. Finally, one woman wrote, "OK, already - I 'hosie' taking her home on Friday and on Monday!" I wrote back asking for an interpretation and if hosie was another cute Maine term I hadn't caught onto yet - like the way everyone uses the phrase wicked good to describe something really cool - I really like that one and have adopted it into my vocabulary. Anyway, she said it meant like when you were a kid and call (claim) the front seat when getting in the car. That really cracked me up!

I enjoyed conversing with the woman who drove me home and to hear about her life. It gave me a new perspective on the whole issue of my working while I'm on the road. While I still believe I will find some other way to make my living while traveling, I have decided what I'm doing now is really not so bad. Working with people who live in the area gives me a whole different perspective than I could have by simply traveling through and being exposed to only RV people. My coworkers have adopted me into their hearts and have made me feel so welcome and have even asked me to stay. I laugh and say that I would except for one thing: I did not buy an RV to stay put, especially not through a Maine winter! At first, they'd chuckle and try telling me it didn't snow there in the winter in order to entice me to stay; eventually they would admit that they totally understood. But these people loved their homes there and the woman who drove me home said she wouldn't leave here for anything - that it was a big enough change for her when she moved from South Portland to Scarborough (about 10 miles).

The chance to work with these people gave me a whole different perspective than I could have by simply traveling through a town and only being exposed to other RVers. I became grateful for this kind of interaction, instead of complaining. Those people

41

demonstrated to me early on that the greatest blessing of my travels has always been to meet and experience such earth angels along the way.

More than anything, with that whole first work experience being so positive, it started everything off on the right foot. It set the stage for changes to come and how I learned not to be afraid of them. This job turned out to be one of my all-time favorites. My coworkers became really good friends and we'd all laugh when they teased me about my Southern accent. I told them I just couldn't understand how they could communicate without the word y'all in their vocabulary. And they would respond with wicked good, *my favorite saying that I first heard there.*

Those people took me into their hearts; they even took me to lunch as a going away present, something I wouldn't have envisioned a firm doing for temps. As much as I enjoyed my time there and even though they told me I was welcome to stay, I knew this Southern gal could not deal with Maine's snow; besides that, I didn't get an RV to stay in one place and my motorhome was screaming at me, "Hey, we've got tires you know!"

In the RV park, while I was outside cleaning out the bins, two local couples walked by and we got to talking for quite a while. They are long-time Mainiacs and it was nice to have the company and conversation. One man especially had the heavy Downeast accent and I had to really strain to understand what he said. We laughed about and shared our various RV travel stories. They got a kick out of our getting lost between here and Salem and the 'translation' problems I experienced trying to get directions.

As anxious as I had become to hit the road, it took me by surprise when I realized how much I was going to miss Maine. When I initially told my mom where we were headed, she asked why I chose to head north to Yankee country. I did have to laugh when I told her later that it was a bit strange to be in a place whose monuments depicted that they thought the right side had won the Civil War instead of mourning the loss like the South did.

From 2001 Journal:

> *Home truly is where the heart is. My heart is still so happy with my lifestyle and I'm glad that I began this when I did. Right now, with all the uncertainty after 9/11 it wouldn't be probably as feasible to begin this sort of lifestyle. Now all I have to do is maintain it.*

Lessons Learned: I learned a lot from my interaction with the great folks I worked with about many things. Sometimes we fear people and cultures different from our own because we equate difference with danger.

When a coworker called me a *bright light on our floor* because we had chatted about her making her own dreams come true, I felt like I was living up to my *Inspiration* job and that was fulfilling to me. If I had given up when that temp agency guy told me my plan wasn't going to work out, I would have lost out on so much.

I also realized that not everyone has the same type of dreams and what one person craves, another person will do anything to avoid. I couldn't really relate to the one woman who said that a 10-mile move was enough for her. I resonate much more with this sentiment: *"Travel as much as you can, as far as you can, as long as you can. Life is not meant to be lived in just one place."*

Another young woman said she couldn't travel like I do because she couldn't give up her furniture. I've never forgotten that. While I seriously try not to be judgmental (and I admit, rarely succeed), I remember thinking then that she was awfully young to be so set in her ways and attached to material things so strongly. I could more easily understand her saying she couldn't stand being away from her family, or that she loved her job, but furniture of all things - that was replaceable. Oh well, if everyone had the same dreams, we'd have a lot harder time making them come true.

If given a choice, I always said I'd rather not have to work; I'd be happy never to have to set foot in another law office again. But looking back on just a few of these jobs that supported my travel habit, there were so many benefits and experiences I had that I would have missed. They turned out to be an important part of the journey themselves, not just a means to an end.

South Carolina (October - December, 2001)

Charleston, South Carolina was where I landed next for work purposes, not only because I wanted to fully explore that beautiful Southern Belle of a city, but the weather was mild enough to spend the winter. I learned I really had to be flexible there because I discovered the job market rates there were about half of what I made in Maine; I panicked until I saw that RV parks were also about half the cost.

Unlike Maine, I wound up having more than one job during the time I was there. Initially, I worried about not having a job from day to day, but it always worked out. My favorite one was at a small firm within a stone's throw from a waterfront park where I could have a picnic lunch. Another time I worked in the historic district and I could stroll the little streets laid with aged brick, window shopping in the quaint old shops and gazing at the amazingly gorgeous historic homes and churches.

In Charleston, we attended a re-enactment of the Battle of Secessionville at one of the most beautiful plantations there, Boone Hall. Even though not real war, the sounds and chaos made it seem way too real to me when thinking of all the lives lost and families forever torn apart.

We took the ferry out to Fort Sumter National Monument. It was a short but wonderful trip with seagulls flying right beside and behind us catching snacks we tossed to them; they amused us with their theatrics and aerial acrobatics. We enjoyed the tour of the fort - it was interesting to stand in the ruins of the first battleground of the Civil War. What was once a three-story structure was virtually decimated and became a dilapidated half-story pile of stones. The guide talked about milestone moments that happen in our lives - those events that precede what ends up in either disaster or glory - Fort Sumter was certainly one of those in our history.

Florida (January - March, 2002)

The next stop was Orlando because the little girl inside of me never got over the dream of going to Disney World. Don and I had a blast and on a later trip, I brought my mom back there and she even cried at the thought of meeting Mickey at her age. I learned so much about dreams during that trip and all the other things you can learn from a man and a mouse.

The whole time I was there, I worked for the coolest female attorney, nicknamed 'Sly' and she made the work days fun with her hilarious sense of humor and work style. I was again a novelty there and I remember someone stopping at my desk and saying, "Are you that lady who just travels around in an RV with no steady job? Everybody's talking about you. I couldn't do that personally, but that is just so cool!"

I didn't really expect much from working in downtown Orlando, but it was nicer than I had envisioned. Lake Eola Park was a nice little retreat with a huge multi-tiered fountain in the middle with swan paddle boats gliding by. I would feed the seagulls and other birds there while I ate lunch on a bench. I really came to appreciate the different environments I experienced while working in different places.

On days off, we thoroughly enjoyed the two days we spent exploring St. Augustine. They couldn't be prouder there of having the oldest of everything - here's the oldest wooden schoolhouse, there's the oldest pharmacy, over there the oldest grocery store - no new and improved claims there. It was fascinating; I got a kick out of seeing how much things have changed, yet how much they really remain the same.

We climbed all over Castillo de San Marcos, the fort built in 1672 by the Spanish to protect St. Augustine from the English. Flagler College began as the Ponce de Leon Hotel in 1888 and

Don and I were both amazed at how detailed the architecture was and how beautifully it has been preserved. We had a blast on the beach feeding the seagulls, but never got up the energy to climb the 200-plus stairs of the oldest lighthouse.

Another Portland – Oregon (September 2002 - March 2003)

After being introduced to the Columbia River Gorge, I knew I wanted to explore more of its many and varied waterfalls and Portland, Oregon looked like a neat place to work.

Since RV parks there are few and far between and nothing was available closer to downtown Portland, Don and I ended up staying in the little outlying town of Troutdale. I still didn't have a towed car at that point and Don had been transporting me, but even though he didn't agree, I thought it was too much of a daily commute for him. So, I started taking the MAX light rail, another first for me. It took about 1-1/2 hours total to get from my door to work, including getting to the Park & Ride lot, the MAX ride, then a 7-block walk to the building. But the whole package of where I worked made it all worthwhile.

My job was at Davis Wright Tremaine in high rise offices with an amazing view of Mt. Hood. After a little trial period, they made it clear I could work there as long as I was in the area, which at that point was just that summer. Although, walking past those windows and looking out at that scenery made it more difficult to be cooped up inside shuffling paper and staring at a computer screen. Yet once again, the people I worked with made all the difference. Even though it didn't start out that long term, I ended up working there through the winter.

Once I met some folks coming back from Alaska and saw their pictures of those mountains, I knew that's where I wanted to go next. It made more sense to me at the time just to stay there instead of going back to spend the winter in Texas. It would save me a lot of travel money, and since they told me I could work there as long as I wanted, I thought it great to be able to save some money for that big trip. Alaska

46

really was the biggest trip of my life. It was of great significance and also relates well to this 'fear less' theme. More about my Alaska adventures in chapter 8.

Even with the long commute, I still loved working in downtown Portland. They have all these neat little parks scattered throughout the historic district with statues everywhere; Pioneer Square is very cool and the park/garden area referred to as the Park Blocks that goes through the university campus made lunches fun and always something to look forward to, particularly in the summertime.

Although Portland is still my favorite city, I would not want to spend another winter there. The weather is too gloomy and my susceptibility toward depression does not work well with it.

When I was getting ready to leave, what the firm did blew me away and had me in tears. The closest people I worked with threw a huge party for me, all bringing an incredible smorgasbord of homemade treats and decadent chocolate on my last day at the job. Best of all, they doled out big hugs to say goodbye and wish me happy future travels.

I was gifted with two bottles of more expensive wine that I am used to from the attorneys that I worked for, with a note from one that read:

> *Malia - Thank you for everything over the last few months. Thank you for your great attitude and willingness to jump right in, thank you for sharing your dream and your wonderful philosophy of life. I wish you well on your journey. You're an inspiring person. Have fun, travel safely, live joyfully, and enjoy. Take care and God bless you.* - Shannon

Now tell me, despite all the jokes to the contrary, that there aren't at least a FEW good lawyers around who are actually also good human beings! I was lucky enough to work for them there.

Savannah, Georgia (March 2007)

My next memorable temporary work job was in Savannah, which had been a quick overnight stop in 2002 when Don and I were on the way from Charleston to Florida. But I was intrigued enough by that glimpse to put Savannah on my list of 'come back to' when I had more time.

That return finally came in March, 2007, after my trip to Alaska. I started by scoping out the area I wanted to work in to get a list of the law firms around there. I was exploring the historic district and walking down this particularly lovely avenue (Oglethorpe) loaded with azalea bushes. And I had the thought, "If I have to work while I'm here, this is where I want it to be." I wanted to be able to walk around and explore the squares during lunch hour and after work. I was standing right at the entrance of the old Colonial Cemetery at that point after being intrigued with some of the stories of the old souls buried there.

The only thing I was afraid of at this point was not having enough time to properly explore the city again when I went back to work. But I got out the phone book and earmarked attorneys that had websites and email. I decided to tackle the task the easy way this time and send inquiries by email instead of going around and leaving resumes in person.

After sending out about a dozen, I remember thinking no way would I get a job that easy and I'd better plan on trekking around town again with resume in tow. Imagine my surprise in the next 15 minutes when I got a return email from an attorney with only the terse message "Call me." I did and then went in the next day for the interview. I told him that in my perfect world I wouldn't start for another two weeks since I just got here and wanted to see Savannah in spring bloom before I settled down to work. Then I'd like to work some weeks part time until mid-June when I was leaving town. He then asked how much I wanted per hour. I told him more than I thought I'd get and he then agreed to every single term I asked for in *my perfect world*.

And that's not even the best part - guess where his office was located? Right across the street from the spot I stood on the week before and said, "This is where I want to work!" Talk about the power of positive thinking!

The other cool historic thing is that the office was in one of four Greek Revival townhouses on *Mary Marshall Row*. These treasures were almost demolished in 1960 for their valuable Savannah grey bricks and marble steps. Conrad Aiken, a Pulitzer Prize winning poet, lived in one of these houses when he was 11 years old. One night he overheard his parents arguing, followed by gunshots. The poor kid found the bodies of his parents, his father having committed suicide after killing his mother. He said he felt haunted by his parents ever since then. Since I was writing an article on "Supernatural Savannah" for *MotorHome Magazine*, this was icing on the cake kinda info. However, I never saw or felt anything out of the ordinary during the time I worked there.

From my Journal (May 2007)

> *It's always a little scary going into a new job and the first couple of days are generally the worst. Then you get a little more comfortable as you get acquainted with the other workers, hearing about their lives and telling them about yours. Doing only temporary work allows you to recreate that experience over and over. While there appears to be some good and bad associated with that, I generally believe it better to be exposed to new experiences that may challenge you as opposed to getting and staying in a rut just because it is easier and more comfortable.*

> *As much as I gripe about having to work, I always enjoy walking around during lunch hours, exploring my new home towns and getting to know the people I work with. I also learned that I will do whatever is necessary to support this travel habit, because there is still nothing I would rather do and despite the periodic panic attacks, I still believe this is what I'm meant to be doing. I still have faith that I will be given every opportunity to keep living this dream.*

On days off, since I had good 'ole Southern roots, I made sure to see the historic squares decked out in azaleas. I always marveled at that row of majestic live oak trees at Wormsloe Historic Site and all those wonderful old Southern homes with the massive porches. I guess a part of me will always be a Southern Belle.

Lessons Learned: I found that just because my original idea of how things would go with temp jobs and how I'd get them didn't work that way, things ultimately worked out better than I thought they could in my initial plans. I chalked up another lesson about fear never being as bad as you imagine it to be. If we can stay open to the possibilities, it can be better than our small minds can even imagine in advance.

Chapter 7
HISTORY LESSONS

It came as a bit of a shock to me that some of the things I enjoyed the most from my years of travel were the historical sites. I guess it was a bit surprising since I found history such a boring subject in school. But being immersed in it was ever so much more interesting, especially things related to the Native Americans. For example, in Oklahoma and Arkansas, I saw how the Cherokee lived happily long before being *civilized*. I walked along the Trail of Tears with tears in my eyes thinking of the Cherokee walking this very path with years of broken promises ringing in their ears.

As for Oregon history, we went to visit the official end of the Oregon Trail Museum and Interpretive Center. I always enjoy those kinds of presentations - they showed you what kinds of wagons were used, the provisions needed and their cost and the kinds of details you generally don't think of because we're so used to modern conveniences. It was very interesting to think of almost 400,000 people during that great emigration period, enduring the hardships necessary to move to an unknown territory and start a new life. This was brought into focus when we saw the presentation about things the pioneers had to leave behind because of weight, size, etc.

There was a school class of pre-teens in our group tour. During one re-enactment, a pioneer woman was unhappy because she couldn't bring her big heirloom bed. One kid from the class asked if they brought along things like the iron stove that was on display and another boy chimed in, "No, that's too heavy - they could just buy another one when they got where they were going." We laughed because we realized that even after the history lesson, he didn't totally get that these people were not going to find a Wal-Mart at the end of the trail - they were the first people there and had to be totally self-sufficient upon arrival. He just hadn't grasped that concept and I realized how foreign that idea is to our modern culture who can find anything we want within relatively easy commuting distance. That's even harder to wrap your mind around when you realize that it was less than 200 years ago and now the hardest thing to imagine is any land left unexplored.

Massachusetts:

After leaf peeping in New Hampshire, we headed into Massachusetts for another lesson in history. We visited Plymouth Plantation, an authentic recreation of the settlement as it existed in 1627. They have set it up as a working village, where crops are grown as they were then, the houses furnished and barns placed as maps showed them to be at the time. There were people playing the parts of the first settlers known to have lived there at the time and their histories. They take this role-playing very seriously in an attempt to truly transport you back into that time period and give you a glimpse of what their lives were like. You visit them inside their houses and out in the fields and they will answer questions about their lives before and after their arrival in Plymouth. They speak in the dialect of the times and it's as close as I've ever come to having my wish come true where I am transported back in time and can truly see what life was like at different times in history.

A while later we took the tour of the recreation of the Mayflower ship at the harbor, I found out it was true when the brochure said they will not speak to you of what they do not know - they will look at you very puzzled if you ask about something beyond the year of 1627 which is what they are recreating. Once I saw what the accommodations were like on the ship that was just 90 feet long and 25 feet wide and that carried 102 total passengers (and a crew of 25), I remarked to one of the female passenger actresses that 32 kids were a lot to handle for 67 days that way. She looked at me strangely and said the baby goats were kept penned with the other animals. I laughed when I realized the term kids for children was not in the vernacular of the period.

We also got to learn a little of the Wampanoag Indian tribe who were here and how they first helped and then later fought the settlers. However, the Indians are not portrayed in the first person the way the settlers were. It was explained that is because there are written journals of the actual settlers and historical data about them. However, the Indians' traditions were all handed down orally and not nearly as much is known about them, at least not from their own perspective of the times.

It was especially telling when we heard one of the settlers make the remark that they thought it good of God to have placed the Indians here for their benefit - like that was their only purpose for being there. No doubt the settlers would have starved that first winter if not for the help of the Indians, but those same settlers still believed that when the diseases they brought that wiped out more than half of the natives, that was Divine Providence - God's way of clearing the land for them - giving them uncontested title in that way. Pretty crude idea of Christianity, huh?

In Boston, we walked down the Freedom Trail, which is a route filled with historical buildings and incredible statues and memorials to our forefathers. We walked through Boston Commons, the oldest public park in America where I encountered the most amazing weeping willows ever. We had lunch at Cheers and then strolled past the oldest graveyard in Boston where Paul Revere is buried.

You never could have convinced me that history was so interesting when I sat at my desk in school fighting to stay awake through class and trying to memorize dates and names of people whom I found boring and irrelevant.

Pennsylvania:

Next on our historical tour, we visited Gettysburg National Cemetery and the National Civil War Museum. Again, actually being at the site of the battle and where Lincoln stood and spoke afterwards, gave a totally different perspective to the history lessons I yawned through in school.

I'm grateful we had the chance to take a more extended tour of the Gettysburg battleground. I did not know how truly beautiful the countryside is where the battle took place. We bought a cassette and map for use as we drove through a self-guided tour of the different landmarks and battle sites. It even had sound effects of the cannons booming through the peaceful landscape and gave me a perspective of the reality of the conflict I had never had before. I never understood the scope of this war or the number of casualties each side suffered.

The more than 1,300 monuments and statues throughout the battlefield make the tour worthwhile. With symbolism and artistry, they memorialize each party's loss in this important battle. They seek to interpret and reconcile the incomprehensible - how brother fought brother in a war in which the enemy was not the feared stranger as in most combats. Before this political clash, we stood side by side against the British so that we could become a united nation. No lofty idealism here - the North may not have been so adamant against it if slavery was as advantageous economically to their industrial culture as it was to the South's agricultural one. And how ironic that the South was fighting for the freedom to enable them to enslave another culture.

Virginia:

Colonial Williamsburg, the capitol of Virginia at the time, was where the idea of patriotism was first conceived. There are acres of original and recreated buildings set up like the town of that period - the gardens, the alleyways, the shops. You get to visit people in their homes and places of business - watch them make the clothing of the period, see how the furniture and other things were made using the tools and techniques of the times. You stroll down streets visiting with people in period costumes, wave to those riding in horse drawn carriages (no cars allowed, of course.) Actors play the parts of the local dignitaries of the day - we got to see them before they were famous! When we were there, they were portraying the summer of 1774. We stood under a huge oak tree listening to George Washington tell us of the proposal to boycott imports from England in response to their closing the harbor as punishment for Boston's little tea party. Patrick Henry, one of the first rebel rousers, was not nearly as moderate in his stand and it was a kick listening to him and his contemporaries in response to his revolutionary ideas. The fear of war and what it would mean to them economically as well as the cost in lives was heavy on their minds and the source of great dissension - that was a little too contemporary for me.

We spent two entire days and still did not see it all - it's an amazing and vast area. More than ever, I felt immersed in the past - watching couples stroll down the canal at the side of the Governor's Palace - the ladies in their long gowns and fashionable hats with their arm in the elbow of the long-coated gentlemen wearing those cute little tights - what a trip!

We participated in a trial of the Virginia Witch - an actual trial that was conducted in that era with testimony from the hysterical townspeople who were sure she had cursed their fields, caused their pigs to go wild and induced a woman's miscarriage - I couldn't tell which upset them more.

New York:

Early on, coming back from Niagara Falls, we camped in a little park in the Adirondack Mountains. By the time I parked *Inspiration* in one of the smallest slots we'd been in so far, there was a crowd gathered around with women cheering that a woman was driving such a huge machine and had parked it so effortlessly. Although she is big, she comes equipped with a backup video camera with audio and I have Don at the side with his now-familiar signals, so under those conditions, it's really not as hard as it would first appear to be.

Actually, that's a perfect analogy for a lot of the problems we create and limitations we set for ourselves - if we would just set about using the help that is all around us, we would accomplish a lot more than we ever suspected we could, if all we looked at were the difficulties and the size of the perceived problems.

Lessons Learned: There's a lot to be learned from history that relates to many areas of our lives each day. I'm glad I had the chance to go back in time in these ways at those incredible sites, especially those that were painstakingly recreated. I think it's also wise to look back at our own lives sometimes for lessons you have learned, but not get stuck in the past and forget that the object in life is to move forward wiser from the experiences!

Chapter 8
ALASKA
The New Frontier

When I decided to become a full-time RVer, I thought I had dealt with the biggest fear imaginable. Even though I drove and lived in my motorhome alone, my best friend, Don, had been alongside me in his Airstream for the first two years; it had provided a safety net that I had come to rely on. Not only did I feel safer, but his company was such a comfort and his sense of humor could make me laugh hysterically, which made every outing more enjoyable.

After spending the winter of 2002 working in Portland to save up enough money for the trip to Alaska in 2003, I was shocked when he told me that it was time for him to return to Texas. My first instinct was to cancel the trip - because no way should I go that far by myself, right?

But Don was his usual inspirational self and assured me that he knew that I most certainly could do that even if I didn't believe it now. But other 'practical' folks were not as encouraging in that regard. Of course, they thought their advice was for my own good so they threw whatever they could think of in my way because all they wanted was to keep me safe. They also argued that at least I should wait until gas prices were lower because at that time, they were at record highs.

However, I didn't need anyone else to tell me how many things could possibly go wrong. I was perfectly capable of sabotaging myself quite effectively. I told myself that it wouldn't be terrible to just hang around the Pacific Northwest area. Lord knows there's enough beauty there to keep me occupied - so I didn't need to go all the way to Alaska.

One of the biggest arguments against going on came down to money; most of my fears usually seem to have to do with finances. At that point, I figured I'd get some kind of temp job, probably in Anchorage during that summer, but there was no guarantee of that. Leaving a sure thing – a good job at a great law firm in beautiful downtown Portland would have certainly kept me more financially stable and made a whole lot more sense if that was the most important consideration.

The thoughts went on and on and swirled around and around - trying to justify playing it safe versus what could be the adventure of a lifetime. Would the idea of a 52-year-old woman driving a 36-foot motorhome and towing a car all the way to Alaska SOLO be crazy and full of scary challenges? Every time I saw pictures of the mountains and the other majestic views waiting there, I just wanted to go so bad that my heart would hurt with the yearning for it. And really, there have been crazier things done in this world by even saner people than me, so I could never believe the thinking that it was impossible, no matter how crazy it might seem to anyone else.

From my Journal (March 14, 2003)

Written while I was still in the decision-making stage and still trying to muster the courage to even get to the planning stage:

> *I spent a lot of time agonizing over the decision, taking into consideration as many points of view as I could think of - and as always, when I analyze things to death, I wind up more torn and confused.*
>
> *In reviewing my old journal entries, I've learned how much I've let my spirits fall and allowed in negative thinking, which are always dream breakers. Even though I have no doubts about this life I've chosen, I've let things like the aches & pains and health concerns I've been experiencing in the past year lead me into obsessive worry, doubt and other invasive negative thoughts. Reading back on how positive and intuitively I started out has made me remember what I want instead of what I've been settling for. It's time to enjoy each day of the trip and keep*

58

looking out the window at the beautiful scenery along the way instead of living in the dark clouds.

The final decision came after much prayer and meditation asking for guidance with the right choice. Very clearly, the first thing that popped into my mind was a question thrown back at me. "What would you do if you had no fear?" I had to laugh because when taken to that basic point, the answer was clear - I wanted to go to Alaska. Maybe it didn't make sense and certainly it didn't sound like a practical choice. But I didn't start this journey to be practical - and if I had let fear rule two years ago I would not have experienced all the wonders I've seen.

Once again, I realized how it always comes back to that question: "What would you do if you had no fear?" So, here's what I concluded on that day in 2003:

I finally decided it was best for me to go on to Alaska now, especially since I had fear surrounding it. It's only when I move through my fear instead of giving in to it that I feel best about myself. And no matter how I justified it, or where else I would go, my not doing what I want to do - what I've dreamed of and worked for during a dismal winter - would feel like giving in and giving up. And especially now, I don't need that drain on my self-esteem. I think it's important for me to know that I truly can do this all by myself at this point in my life. When I'm torn between feeling proud of myself for taking such a risk (as full time RVing can be), I recognized and embraced the feelings of terror because I'm not employed at a stable job building a retirement fund with full insurance benefits, etc. But this is my choice and I absolutely have no regrets for allowing myself this dream. So, I guess the best way to do it is with as much of a full-tilt-boogie attitude as possible.

I usually do come up with something to convince myself to do what I want to do even if I have to play mind games to get there. I told myself it's all a matter of perspective anyway. It's 2,500 miles from where I am now to Anchorage. It's about the same from where I am now back to Austin. So basically, I'm halfway to Alaska anyway and it would be a shame to turn back now, don't you think?

It's only when I move through my fear instead of giving in to it that I feel best about myself, became a sort of mantra for me. When I had that thought during the decision-making process, I felt a shiver go through me; an indication I take as being inspired by a higher thought than I am sometimes capable of on my own. I had that same shiver reading it today.

Lessons Learned: Always trust yourself over others - even those you love and who love you aren't always right when it comes to what is best for you. It's not always wise to wait for a better day since that day may not come. I looked back at my notes and saw that when I left Olympic, Washington on May 3, 2003, I paid $1.74 per gallon of gas. In 2018, we know we'll never see prices that low again. Fears like to multiply themselves. When we are trying to make one decision, a lot of other, even unrelated fears become even scarier and yell for equal attention. They may be hard to disregard but if you listen to any one of them, you're a goner.

Even after the decision was made to actually spend the summer traveling around Alaska on my own, it certainly didn't stop the fear and doubts. But I was getting practice at working around them.

British Columbia, the Good that Made all the Bad Worthwhile:

Regardless of the collection of fears in planning and actually getting to Alaska, along the way there were plenty of times that truly fit the bill of *once in a lifetime*. The most memorable and magical happened in British Columbia when I pulled off alongside Muncho Lake to take a break and just take in the view. The lake was still frozen and covered in snow in places and was the most incredible color of blue I had ever seen. Across the lake were glacier-capped mountains with waterfalls tumbling into the lake.

Muncho Lake Journal (May 8, 2003)

Even though this was very early in the trip, this stop was one of the most memorable moments for me - not only of this trip, but in my entire life.

There was no one else around and I was just standing there gazing in awe when I became aware of a cracking sound. At first it was almost imperceptible as the snowy white silence seemed complete. I couldn't figure out what it was and it had me a little nervous. I walked around and inspected Inspiration (my motorhome) and then realized what I was hearing was the sound of the lake melting beside me! When I looked closely, I could see the subtle shifts in the water and the thin ice covering near the shore giving way to spring. I then literally dropped to my knees in tears - it moved me almost more than I could say. Even now, I don't really know how to explain it. I just sobbed like a baby, saying over and over to myself, 'You're hearing the lake melting - and look at that, and look at that - you can even see it melting!'

It was one of the most cosmic, magical moments in my entire trip. Who would have ever thought the sound of ice melting could be magical, but I assure you it was.

I saw my first moose alongside that road; near Liard Hot Springs, I had a deer run alongside and in front of me for quite a while, like she was leading me, saying "Isn't this just great?" Since the deer is my totem animal, I considered this a particularly good sign.

Reading back over those journal entries, I am so grateful for the encouragement of people who cared, some of whom I hadn't even met at that point. We all have the ability to make a huge difference in the life of another. My goal is to do whatever I can to pay that kind of kindness (and inspiration) forward.

On May 14, 2003, I was almost there and wrote:

Tomorrow I will finally be in Alaska! I can't believe it's been a little less than a month since I left Portland. In some regards it feels like a lifetime. In some ways it's been a much harder month of travel than I had ever imagined and in other ways I am amazed at how smooth it went. My emotions have certainly run the gamut, that's for sure. From the loss of my greatest inspiration, Don - to a feeling of accomplishment that I've come so far alone - to doubting the wisdom of ever taking off on such a crazy and risky dream - to being totally and unbelievably excited at the prospect of spending the whole summer in amazing Alaska - I've experienced it all. If one of the things that life is all about is to experience and learn as much about ourselves and others as we can during our time on earth, then I feel like I've lived a lifetime just in the past month. Being the only one to listen to myself cry in fear and frustration or sob in joy and wonder - in that experience, I've learned a lot about myself.

Reading back over that old 2003 journal in 2018 also reminded me how much has changed and that what I was doing then was much less common than it is now:

I know I'm not the only single woman RVer who has ever made the trip through here, but you would think so with the reactions I get from most of the people I've met along the way. Mostly it's the women who are amazed as they vow they could never do such a thing. I beg to differ since I can be found just as guilty as anyone of doubting myself, so I firmly believe that if I can, anyone can follow their dreams if they have the desire and determination.

I arrived in Alaska the next day:

Alaska at Last! It was crying-with-joy-time again when I saw the 'Welcome to Alaska' sign. I made it!

My first long stop was Valdez and since I arrived so early in the season, the RV park owner allowed me to park lengthwise so that my entire side was waterfront with views like I had never seen in my life.

While sitting on a bench one day, I could see a light mist approaching and all of a sudden, I was enveloped by it. I shivered all over with pleasure as I realized that I was being kissed by a cloud! It felt like it passed right through me as it gently moved on. It was a blessing unlike anything I ever imagined. I've forgotten a lot of things in my life, but I'll never forgot the sweetness of a cloud kiss and I'm eternally grateful I got to experience it. I've heard that particular RV park no longer exists, so I would have missed so much if I had waited for a better time.

I had a bear in my backyard while staying in Anchorage and my neighbor took a picture of me with him in the background. On the way back home one night, I laughed out loud at the cottonwood balls that looked like snow flying into my windshield. And I laughed at the fact that I needed sunglasses at 10:30 at night because the sun was still bright and setting in my face.

I could have taken a hundred pictures a day just showing the play of the light, clouds and shadows moving across the snow-capped mountains. Sometimes I would just sit in awe, telling myself, "I did it - I'm really in Alaska!" I was thrilled to see a bald eagle flying over my house - even more so when I managed to get a picture of him.

Although there are some people I met there who I'm still in contact with in some way, even if just on Facebook, I've never again seen or talked to most of the people I met in Alaska that summer. But so many touched my heart then, so here are some of the things I wrote back then that I still cherish today:

> *Good or bad, it definitely is a different dynamic being alone here. People seem to relate to me differently - or maybe it's just me that is relating differently, who knows? RV people have always been nice and helpful, but they seem especially so now, after*

finding out I'm on my own. That feels pretty good and is somehow comforting.

It was nice getting all the email I received. Being alone makes keeping in contact with my friends all the more important. I wonder if they realize how much their words of encouragement mean to me. I wonder if they know how much I am heartened by the words of wisdom I receive from those that take the time to let me know they are thinking of me and are with me in spirit.

Part of the miracle of this journey for me has been the lessons I have learned from the people I've been blessed to meet. So often we take it for granted that the people who come into our lives come simply by happenstance, by accident. One of the basic tenets of metaphysics says there are no accidents and that everything happens for a purpose. God knows that since I talk to rocks and believe mountains are alive, it is no surprise that I believe strongly that every single person I meet, especially in this type of journey, carries with them a gift for me - and vice versa. I've had the term inspiration come up so much in the way people describe their reaction to what I'm doing. But all along the way, that's exactly what I've gotten from the people I've met along the road.

Woody and Genie married for 47 years and still obviously in love - what an inspiration for me, a charter member of the Cynical About Lasting Love Ever Being Possible Club. The way they took me under their wings and kept me informed of road conditions and other useful info as they paved the way — made them a true joy to be around. Chuck and Kalyn loving their traveling lifestyle and each other - I just instantly felt comfortable with them like I'd known them for years and by the time my mom joined me for the return trip, they had become my adopted siblings.

It's been great fun to run into them along the road and no doubt we'll meet again. As big as Alaska is, we Texans can't seem not to meet each other out here.

Just a few days later, though, in one of the prettiest places I've ever seen in my life, I was again haunted by fear and doubt:

64

I've noticed since I've been here in Valdez that the weather and the glorious views have consistently been great - it's only my moods that shift the perception of them. Sometimes I look out my window and cry in happy wonder of it all - sometimes I cry in wonder of what in the hell I'm doing so far from home (wherever that is) all alone in the wilderness. Nothing else has changed - no outside force or danger has presented itself - it's only my mind playing games and bringing every emotion out to play. I remember reading that Alaska is still a wild place in many ways and that's the draw for some people. But it's not a place to hide because nature and the forces here are so powerful that it won't let you get away with that. The enormity of the mountains can make you feel small and insignificant or make you feel larger than life when you realize you are part of and connected to everything in ways our minds just cannot grasp most of the time.

So, when I get the blues or a bad case of the doubts, I try to wait it out with the knowledge that "this too shall pass." And the mountains will wait until I can see them with a lighter heart and the sea will still sparkle when my eyes aren't wet with tears. Since waiting for anything is not my strong suit, I was so struck with the words of a Sarah McLachlan song, "Wait for the Way," that just popped up with perfect timing.

I'm officially the world's most impatient person, so that was a tough one for me, but the thought of turning back at that point, was more terrifying than anything else! And the wait is always worthwhile when the good comes around to more than offset the bad.

Then there were times on the road that I'd either be going up or down a mountain pass and already start dreading it going back. If I was going up and it was steep and I still made it okay without overheating or any other problems, I'd worry about what it would be like going the other way and if I'd lose control going down such a steep grade.

While I was in Anchorage, it turned out I could not find temporary work and began to worry about dwindling funds.

So, I took off to the incomparable Russian River, a place that became special to me in more ways than one. When I originally planned the trip to Alaska, I decided that I wouldn't stay in out-of-the-way parks, even though they were much more scenic. I just didn't think I'd feel as safe there, as I did when Don was parked right beside me. Well, I did that anyway; I considered it a victory to overcome the limitations I had placed on myself due to fear.

But as I was leaving there, these fears surfaced:

> *Somehow I almost feel like a little kid that's being let loose on the world and who doesn't quite feel prepared for that giant leap. A part of me feels like retreating back into more familiar, known territory. I think about going back to Anchorage and trying again to get some work for a while, just to feel 'normal' again. It's odd that I almost can't relate to being this free, especially when part of me did not want to work anyway. It is interesting that I find myself looking for ways to feel more confined, as if that offers more security, because that is what I am most familiar with.*

Even though my plan to work in Anchorage at least some during that summer didn't work out, just looking for it resulted in a great meeting I journaled about:

> *When I got to Anchorage, I made attempts to get that temp work I told myself I needed during the planning stages. Turns out summer is not the best time to get temp work in Anchorage since most people take their vacations to escape there during the winter.*

> *But I'll never forget a woman I met at one of the prospective law offices. After I introduced myself to Barbara, the receptionist, she took a look at my card and read the first few sentences of my introductory letter and was immediately intrigued. As we discussed how I worked to support myself as I go, I said it was my dream to travel and this was the only way I could figure out how to do it. We laughed as we almost said at the same time, "all it took was a giant leap of faith." She confided that her dream was to further her divinity education and we agreed that*

66

it is so easy to get caught up in fear and put limitations on ourselves that we neglect our dreams out of a need to feel safe and secure, like the two things somehow must be mutually exclusive.

Anyway, it was worth the whole effort of getting up early, getting dressed up and hitting the streets to solicit work I really didn't want to do, just so I could meet that woman. I still remember my favorite thing she said, "When I'm hit with a challenge, I just pray, 'Well, Lord, what are you going to do with this one to have it turn out for my good?' When she said I had been an inspiration to her and that she considered my message as one from God that she should pursue her own dream, I couldn't help but hug her and we both got a little teary-eyed. It was quite a moving moment and a pretty cool thing to happen on my first full day in Anchorage.

Lessons Learned: Thankfully, most of the collection of fears I had before taking off were not really deserving of the worry and fear I inflicted upon myself. Likewise, the fears that popped up along the way were never as dark nor the mountains as steep as I had feared.

Even though it turned out that I never did get a job in Anchorage, I never went hungry or ran out of gas and always had a place to park my home. So even when you think a part of the plan is definitely necessary, if it doesn't work out exactly that way, doesn't mean the whole idea is doomed.

I may have given in to tears and fears sometimes, but I still appreciate this summation: "And despite it all, I'm still willing to trade security for adventure." And miracles and angels were all around me then and now. My trip to Alaska is one of the life experiences I accomplished that I'm still very proud of all these years later.

Chapter 9

WHO THREW THAT MONKEY WRENCH?

For the past 17 years, I've gotten emails and messages from people telling me how inspired they are by what I've done. Sometimes I think if they only knew the insecurity I felt inside, they would judge me to be a fraud. I am not always brave, often scared, insecure, angry, uncertain, second guessing myself at every turn. Guess what? That is a normal process if you're going to grow and not stay stagnant. Sometimes the going was pretty rough; I include some of my old journaling to show how I was dealing with it all then. Even after I was on the road for a couple of years, proving to myself that I could do it, the doubts and fears would still pop out from the dark places in my mind.

I can still easily get down on myself, but I try to give myself credit for not simply giving up during hard times. Like a friend told me when people tell her how brave she is to full-time RV alone, "I am not brave - I am determined!"

From Journal – 2003 - Renting my House Versus Selling:

> *Back in Austin – 2003: I've been back in Austin less than three weeks, but already it has surpassed the welcome home I received last year. Coming back here last March, for the first time since I started full-time RVing, was a difficult experience that resulted in me alternating between anxiety, fear and depression. I had more trouble and expense finding another tenant for my house, as the job and real estate market in Austin had tumbled following 9/11. The reduced rent I received was no longer fully paying my mortgage and RV payments, which was what helped make it possible for me to travel full-time.*

This stress, along with the death of my father, sent me into 'worry-land' and that's never a pretty place to be. Even though I found a job relatively quickly, the pay wasn't as good as I expected and financial worries can be very ugly.

There were times when I feared I wouldn't be able to get away from Austin again - that something would happen to make me have to stay there. What a relief when the house was rented again to a great tenant and Don and I escaped again in July of last year. I thought that had taught me the lesson that all things do truly happen as they should and that worry is useless to say the least, but I'm definitely revisiting that lesson now for sure. In some of the panicky dreams I've had throughout my life, I feel like a schoolgirl not ready for the big test and feeling naked going through the hall; even if no one else notices, I feel so self-conscious and vulnerable.

Last summer in the Pacific Northwest was stellar and this past summer in Alaska should have proven to me that I can pull this off. I need to have a little more faith in myself and in the ultimate goodness of the universe. I still haven't quite found that key, because here I am worried again and in a general state of anxiety. My house now sits vacant again since my great tenant got married and I'm told I'll have to reduce the rent even further because lower interest rates have people who used to pay high rent, buying homes of their own.

I was able to get a great paying job pretty quickly though, so I'm trying hard not to freak out too much about the house sitting vacant for at least a month as of now.

In the spirit of the sage advice, 'even if you don't know the exact next step, stop doing what isn't working,' I'm ready to let go of the fear or to walk around it. Whatever it is, whatever the reason for the fear, whether it would make more sense or be 'prudent' and stay in one place, I'm still going to start taking those baby steps again toward my own dreams.

Lessons Learned: Despite the presence of fear throughout the process and things certainly not always going as I envisioned they would, all those baby steps carried me

69

through. I was able to pull it all off and stay on the road since 2001. I may not have an abundance of financial or spiritual reserves, but things seem to come as needed right in time. The bottom line is: there are tradeoffs. Sometimes you have to give up *stuff* to get the more important things that you really want.

Alaska Anxiety:

My summer in Alaska was the perfect example of expectations of things always going perfectly being unrealistic. Even though my adventures in the Alaskan and Canadian wilderness had been filled with wonderful experiences and lessons, there always comes a time when it seems someone has literally thrown a monkey wrench into even the best laid plans.

My rational mind understands that I can't expect to drive a motorhome 5,000 miles up mountainous terrain and not incur some repair costs. For some reason, however, whenever I am faced with an unexpected repair bill, my first mode of operation is to freak out in panic.

At some point, I comfort myself with how much worse it could have been. It usually takes me longer to recognize the *silver linings* - the unexpected blessings that happened as a result of what I considered to be a curse at the time. When I look back on that whole summer, when things came up, I was able to handle them all pretty quickly and relatively inexpensively.

Of course, I had everything checked out and maintenance done before I left. But even though the heater and generator were included in that service, those were the things I had the most issues with, both necessities when traveling through Alaska.

During an overnight at the Wal-Mart in Whitehorse, it was the coldest and windiest weather of the trip thus far. I had a rude awakening at 1 a.m. - totally freezing with nothing but cold air coming from my propane furnace. I had no idea what to do, so I turned everything off and went back to bed with my long johns on and comforter around me. I tossed and turned the rest of the night totally worried about what was wrong and how much it would cost. I probably wouldn't be able to find a repair place way out here…and on and on with the fear and doubt.

When I called the manufacturer, it turned out there was a certified repair shop less than two blocks from me. And they were kind enough to drop everything and work on it right then. They finally determined that it was a minor adjustment that hadn't been made correctly when the circuit board was replaced before I left. Another $150 later (much better than my nightmares made me think it would be) and I was on the road - warm again. If it had happened earlier when I really was out in the middle of nowhere, it certainly would have been a more serious situation.

Since I had heard about the great scenic boondocking spots around Alaska, I made sure I had the generator serviced before I left. But when I was on the incredible Homer Spit in dire need of coffee that morning, it turned on, but electricity wasn't actually getting to the motorhome. The manufacturer basically said it could be a simple connection or something more involved that could require replacing. Of course, that sent me into a complete tizzy, imagining the worst-case scenario. In my panic, I quickly thought, I can't afford a new generator, I'm out in the middle of some damn spit in Alaska; what in the hell was I thinking that I should do this crazy trip? After driving myself frantic, that time I found a mobile repairman. It ended up being a minor thing that cost me all of $180 to fix…and I still had the nerve to gripe about that!

While boondocking at the Russian River, I discovered my house batteries wouldn't hold a charge and I had to get them replaced on my next stop in Anchorage. I found a good battery place having a sale on the golf cart style that was better anyway, so again, I couldn't complain too much about that.

But when I discovered my new point and shoot HP camera quit working and pictures were out of focus no matter what I did, I was stressed to the max. I was in tiny Valdez at the time in one of the most scenic spots I had ever seen and the thought of not taking pictures was unimaginable!

When I reached HP on the phone, they said that error message was 'unresolvable' and I'd have to send the camera in for repair, which would take 6 to 8 weeks. Obviously, that wasn't going to work in this case and when I explained that I was on a once-in-a-lifetime Alaska vacation, she took pity and sent me a new camera by FedEx. Tell me that wasn't an angel and a miracle all wrapped into one!

But the mishap that cracked me up the most (literally and figuratively) happened one morning in Valdez after breakfast while I was cleaning the coffee pot. I had the thought, "I'd hate to break my pot now and have to try to find one in this little town." I swear it wasn't two seconds later…while rinsing it, I hit it against the sink and heard that sick breaking glass sound. I just could not believe it! But I had to laugh in gratitude that not everything I fear comes to me that fast and furious! I found a Safeway that had one little 4-cup Mr. Coffee that cost a ridiculous amount of money, but at least I didn't have to give up my coffee. That would most definitely be too big a fear for me to conquer.

While I was reliving these events, what struck me the most was how blessed I was that people (I say they are really angels in human form) always showed up to help me get through them. These problems were handled in ways I couldn't have imagined at the time.

Once when I went into an RV park office to check in after dealing with one problem or another, the lady greeted me and asked how I was doing. I'm sure she didn't expect me to burst into tears in response, but that's exactly what I did. I blubbered about the day I'd had and felt like a fool when I just couldn't stop. She didn't look at me like I was crazy, but literally came over and took me into her arms and comforted me. I told her how my friends and family all either thought I was very brave or very stupid to be taking this trip alone and right now I was siding with the extremely stupid consensus. She told me that of course sometimes unexpected things happen, but in the end, these things can make us stronger and more resilient. She said to remember that I was doing what I was supposed to be doing and this was an adventure of a lifetime that I will never regret having done. She reminded me that I proved that I can handle problems as they come up and that it's okay to have a good cleansing cry now and then.

Having these unexpected confirmations and consolations were invaluable at the time, but I confess that it still didn't keep me from future meltdowns and spiritual breakdowns.

> *It didn't matter how much I had learned about what I was capable of - there was no weight given to what I had already been through. I had never felt so alone, isolated or vulnerable. I was tired of having to deal with the seemingly constant things going wrong with the RV and the time and money it takes to do the repairs.*

> *Like Dorothy in the Wizard of Oz, I felt trapped in a distant foreign land; I just kept thinking, "I want to go home - I'm scared and I'm so tired and I just want to go home!" These situations were the only times I questioned my decision to go to Alaska. The only catch is my home is with me and there really is nowhere else I feel the sanctuary of safety I was looking for anyway.*

So, there were plenty of times when I felt incapable of continuing with even a hint of bravery, but continue I did, even when I felt a sense of failure for still being so afraid:

> *Sometimes I think I must be crazy that I just can't seem to relax without all the drama. Crying in awe of the beauty that surrounds me is far easier for me to understand than me sobbing sadly for unknown reasons or crying uncontrollably over a repair bill. Why do I create such tension in myself for no good apparent reason? I find myself wondering what in the hell I'm doing in the middle of the Yukon all by myself and then I*

realize I'm not really by myself at all. Just as from the beginning of this journey, God continues to send me nothing but miracles and angels.

It didn't always take physical meetings to remind me of big truths. My very intuitive friend, Steph, wrote in response to one of my 'woe is me' updates and what I thought about that:

You probably don't want to hear this, but you know me, I will say it anyway. I think you are really missing the companionship you shared with Don. He was always there to share your excitement and such beautiful places. You had him by your side for many miles and always felt safe. I know you are safe there, lock your doors, pull your shades, have a few drinks, and enjoy! And remember, you are actually doing what most people only dream about.

She was so right on the money that it is scary! I'm sure a lot of the emotional upheavals I feel stem at least in part from the ever-so-present sense of loss when he is not with me to share the beauty I am seeing and that I know he would love so much. But I do take comfort in the knowledge that I absolutely still do feel that I am doing what I am supposed to be doing. If I could just stop judging my reactions and emotions, I'd probably be a whole lot more comfortable and relaxed.

Sweet Judith answered my whiney, "Why?" questions, with:

Why? Why and Why? You feel some of those feelings at times because my dear friend, you are human, you have undertaken an exciting and difficult at times, task, but not without the humanness attached. Stop being so hard on yourself and lighten up - be moody, be sad, be happy, be glad...cry...laugh...feel insecure (just don't dwell in it). It's all a part of who you are, which is pretty wonderful I might add. Thinking of you and sending energy as I write

Although I recognized it even then, that didn't stop me from bitching about one thing or another in my journal:

Now with friends such as these, you would think I'd quit bitching so much, wouldn't you? I am thankful, Spirit, truly I am…it's just that no one, including me, would know it sometimes, that's all.

Sometimes, I am amazed at how flimsy the construction is on these expensive motor homes - and other times I'm amazed at how far this rolling contraption has taken me and I'm grateful for all the things I've gotten to see because of it. I guess that's yet another analogy for my own life and the fear and gratitude I experience on a daily basis. Now if I could just admit more of the gratitude and less of the fear, I'm sure I'd be in much better shape all the way around!

More Troubles and Funnies:

The effort of thinking positive - especially when all the *what ifs* and *if onlys* rear their ugly heads - can be exhausting. There are often dark thoughts and not all sunny days.

One night, the door to my laundry inset in the RV came apart. I guess the vibration of the washing machine with the door left open loosened the frame that held the dozens of little slats. Some were still in place, but some were dangling from one end or the other. When I would get one slat in place, none of the other ones were cooperating. I asked myself why this had to happen now of all times - I didn't have the time, energy or money to deal with another problem, no matter how trivial! I'm embarrassed to admit I sat on the floor and started bawling, emotionally overwhelmed having just left mom being cared for in the hospital. And the thought just popped into my head, "How is this a perfect mirror of my life right now?" Sometimes I do feel that all the slats of my life that I thought were secure are now coming apart and I feel like I have no clue how to get them all back in line. The motorhome is getting older and needs expensive maintenance and repairs - another mirror to my own body and health that is also in need of maintenance.

When I get freaked out because of some unexpected problem or repair and think that maybe it's time for me to settle down in a *real* house, I've been reminded that problems and unexpected things come up no matter where you live or what you live in.

Lost Nut:

As for trying to anticipate and prepare for every detail to keep the bad stuff from happening, who would have thought I'd have a lug nut from a passing truck go through my motorhome windshield and for a second, make me think I had been shot? That was certainly something I didn't have on my list! As I was almost stopped, preparing to make a left-hand turn into a campground in West Yellowstone, a passing truck lost his nut and it found its way straight to my chest after cracking the windshield. In the flash of a second, I saw the hole in the windshield, felt some pressure to my chest, looked down and saw glass covering my arms and lap and wondered why there was no blood. I don't know how I did not panic at that point. Sometimes Jesus really does take the wheel because I made the turn and actually drove around the campground looking for an open site. When I saw people preparing to vacate one, I stopped to ask if I could take that site. The lady came up and looked at my windshield and exclaimed, "You drive around like that!?"

That's about the time I fell into her arms as I was about to crumble to the ground. I assured her it had just happened and I guess I was still in a bit of shock. All I knew at that moment was that I wanted to have a safe place to park. And it turned into another great example of the kindness of strangers. That woman took me over to the host to pay for the site and made sure I was set up properly. When I found out from the insurance company how long it might take to get another windshield installed, the host said I could have the site as long as I needed even though there is normally a one week maximum. Accompanying blessing: I had a great site with electricity in West Yellowstone (it was peak season, so it is normally hard to get into) as my home base from which to explore that amazing park.

Like some kind of cosmic joke, though, while I was exploring around in my little car, a speeding truck coming toward me in a construction zone threw up a rock and cracked that windshield too! I was like, "Come on Universe - seriously now?" But the same guy who fixed the motorhome also fixed the car, so it all worked out.

However, the old Universe had yet another trick up its sleeve. When I discovered the windshield wiper fluid wouldn't come up to clean the windshield, I took it to the dealer to get fixed under warranty. They finally discovered the problem: a mouse had crawled into the fluid reservoir, had decayed and its parts were clogging up the works! The mechanic said everybody out in the bay gagged when they removed it. Since my warranty didn't cover such a sad situation, that was another unexpected expense to gripe about.

Can you be prepared for weird stuff like this? You must be psychic if you can. But there are still ways to deal with issues that arise. And again, help also arrives in ways you can't predict.

The Funnies: When we were *Mainiacs*

I don't know what I would have done without Don by my side at the beginning, but we had our share of mishaps or miscommunications.

The trip to Maine took Don and I more than twice as long as it should have from where we were. Since all the campgrounds and reasonable hotels were full due to a holiday, we decided to take advantage of having fully self-contained units and dry camp at the Walmart in Salem, where at least the price was right. Don led the way in his truck so we'd have transportation around town. Anyway, at some point while we were circling Salem for the zillionth time looking for Wal-Mart, I got separated from him. Those little New England streets are not exactly conducive for a 36 foot motor home to maneuver, especially when you're not sure where to turn, etc. It all turned out okay and in fact, it was kind of funny when it was all over. I wound up about 10 miles away before I could stop in a parking lot of a mall. I stopped a couple of nice ladies to ask where I was and called Don on the cell phone so we could find each other. As she was giving directions, I had a hard time understanding her because of her accent. I was trying to repeat what she said to Don and started spelling some of the streets, joking that since they didn't pronounce their r's that I had to resort to that. The other lady laughed and said, "If you want correct directions, you better not make fun of the way we talk." The lady talking to Don said, "When you pull up in the Staples parking lot, you won't be able to miss the lady in the huge motor home who talks funny." All in all, it was great to meet those 'angels' and add another 'don't do again' to my list. From now on, I will have my own explicit directions to where we're going, no matter how seemingly short the trip. It was silly to just take off believing I could just follow him.

Here's another important tip: If you travel with someone, together or separately, take my advice; go with someone that makes you laugh! It can make all the difference in the world in relieving stress and making it an enjoyable adventure.

I have never laughed so hard in my life than when I was traveling beside Don. He had the zaniest sense of humor and a way of making me laugh so hard I could barely stand up. There were times as we quipped back and forth on the CB, that I'd have to pull over because I was laughing so hard I was crying at what I refer to as his *Don-isms*!

Don had his own special difficulties in communication sometimes. When he asked a lady if she could direct him to a *washeteria*, she looked at him very puzzled and said, "a what?" He repeated himself and he could tell she was trying to be helpful but had no clue what he was talking about. He resorted to slowly enunciating the word (waash-a-teer-ee-ah) but still got the dumbfounded look. He finally said, "the place where you wash your clothes." The light dawned and she exclaimed, "Oh, you mean the Laun-dro-mat" and then proceeded to give directions. To her credit, she didn't laugh until he was out of earshot.

When he was at the gas station, Don thought the man asked him if he had his *cod*. Since he was not at the fish *maahket*, he wondered if they were giving away free fish with gas or something. (That would not be out of the realm of possibility there in Maine.) He finally understood that the man was asking for his credit *card*.

The last time we fell all over ourselves laughing at a mispronunciation, it was Don's own special brand. We were in an aromatherapy store in Freeport and I asked him to read a bottle's label to me since I didn't have my glasses. He started reading the ingredients, and then got to the most important one -- which he pronounced *pot-pour-ee*. I almost choked laughing while asking if that was a version of potpourri. We got a good case of the giggles at that point and couldn't stop. We then saw a big display sign for the new line of "Harbor Mist" products. I wondered aloud what Harbor Mist smelled like. Don theorized that it probably smelled a little like seagull shit. We had to leave the store at that point because we were afraid we'd be kicked out for excessive raucous laughter. A man we passed at the door asked for a sample of what we were smoking.

Another *Don-ism* had me near rolling in the aisles of Bed, Bath & Beyond. We were passing the kitchen supplies and I was walking ahead of him. I heard him say, "Look at that - a spoon rest - I've never heard of a spoon rest before." I just let that pass when he then said, "What about the forks and knives? Those babies have been around a while and get mighty tired, too." Now, him worrying about those poor neglected knives and forks and wondering why they didn't have their own rests just cracked me up and again, I'm sitting here with tears of laughter rolling down my cheeks just thinking about how he said it; I guess it was a case of *you had to be there* and I'm glad I was, even if I can't possibly explain what was so hilarious about that to me.

Of course, I had my own struggles with language and accents. It was funny to hear the Yankee newscasters being entertained by us pitiful Southerners battling those half-inch

79

drifts and poking fun at us for having closed the schools and public buildings for such a light snow shower. Well, I enjoyed our little flurries - it was quite wonderful to see the tiny flakes floating softly through the air only to disappear when earthbound.

Lessons Learned: I have often consoled myself with the knowledge that God doesn't give me more than I can bear; whenever I've had flat tires, it wasn't when I was driving. You can read all you want about what to do in case of a tire blowout - don't slam on brakes, don't overcompensate, etc. - but what really matters is what you remember at the moment it is actually needed.

Another thing I learned was about making judgments. Sometimes what you think is negative actually turns out to be positive. My first time down the Blue Ridge Parkway in the winter of 2002, I was whining that it would be so much better if it were spring when the trees were budding or summer when the trees were full or fall when the trees were colored - anytime other than winter time when they were bare. But then I shut up and began to appreciate what was before me at the time it was there. The trees being stripped of leaves afforded a view through the branches of the far distant mountains and waterfalls that popped up that would not have been visible were they full of leaves. The shadows that the twisted branches cast on the trunks of other trees lent visual interest at every turn. Since we had just gotten a good rain the day before, the huge rock formations shimmered with thousands of little waterfalls alongside the road. We drove beneath clouds, then through them, then on top of them. At the highest peak we reached, the trees were covered with ice making crystal sculptures of every twisted, naked branch and icicles dripped off the myriad of tunnels as we drove right through the mountains.

I don't remember where I read this, but I saved it because I knew I'd need to hear it over and over again:

It is true that life is not always what we want it to be,
but it always and in all ways, gives us a chance to grow and become
something more than we had previously been.
So - when a door closes in your face, shed your tears,
but then turn your head toward the light and you will see
it is coming from a new door that is already opening for you.

Too many of us are not living our dreams
because we are living our fears.

- Les Brown

Part 3

Fearing Less

Chapter 10
FEAR AS OPPORTUNITY

Never fear - there's never a shortage of things of which to be afraid. There are many varieties and reasons for fear when it pops up in our lives. But fear can serve a positive purpose in our lives. Sometimes it appears to keep us safe and from making foolish daredevil choices. Some kinds of fear always seem to come into play when we're contemplating or are forced to make changes in our lives. So - fear can keep us safe or create a catalyst to push us forward. It gives us the opportunity to analyze what is causing the fear and find a positive way to push through it. Trying to ignore your fears will do no good whatsoever. They will keep reoccurring until we pay attention - enough to get the lesson and instructions that come with that particular fear.

I often get emails from women saying they'd do the kind of travel that I do in a New York minute if they were only as brave and fearless as I am. I always assure them that their fears are normal, but it doesn't mean that it has to stop you in your tracks. I tell the complete truth in hopes they'll see themselves in my experiences and try to push past their own fears. You betcha I'm scared sometimes - the full on shaking-in-my-boots kind of scared. No matter how long I have been on the road, I still get butterflies in my stomach when I first get behind the wheel of this big motorhome, especially when it has been parked for a while. It is natural to have some fear whenever you are tasked with the handling of such a big beast. Initially, it feels intimidating, but the fact that nothing bad, drastic or earth-shattering has happened all this time tells me that it really is all good…yet I still feel fear. I call those *reasonable* fears - the kind of things I think are beneficial to be as prepared as you can be beforehand.

Some kinds of fear come up for our protection to keep us from jumping off a cliff, for example. And some are meant to be pushed past, so that we DO take a leap of faith. (Not that I am saying go jump off a cliff, y'all!) Fear can be a good thing when it keeps us on our toes. In that way, we don't ever become complacent and take anything for granted.

Sometimes when I feel fear about something I really want to do, I recite a line from one of my favorite books, *A Tree Full of Angels: Seeing the Holy in the Ordinary*.

> *When we walk to the edge of all the light we have*
> *and take that step into the darkness of the unknown,*
> *we must believe that one of two things will happen...*
> *there will be something solid for us to stand on,*
> *or we will be taught to fly.*

And then for good measure, I chant a quote from Brendan Francis:

> *Many of our fears are tissue paper thin*
> *and a single courageous step would carry us clear through them.*

So, do I take measures to limit putting myself in physical danger? Of course; I may be crazy but I'm not stupid. When it comes to following my dreams of travel, I walk right to the edge of the cliff and look at all the possibilities that exist out there to help my dreams come true. And then positive things start happening in ways I could never have foreseen even before I take that first little step to move me forward. I suggest putting a reasonable limit on your fears. Don't just accept it because something stirs a little fear in you that you shouldn't do it. Fly.

If you think it's okay to wait until you have all your ducks in a row - when you have more free time - when you're caught up with everything and have a big fat pension fund, good luck with that. I've seen many more sad examples of people who tried to do that only to have a major illness or death put an end to the dreams that they worked so hard for.

Don't reach for Fearless. That can be intimidating and make you feel it's impossible. Don't beat yourself up just because you feel afraid or fear will win out. It won't, but inaction will. Just fear *less*. You don't have to eat it all in one bite, you don't have to jump a mile in one leap. Don't fall into the trap of comparing yourself to others. Believe me, the people you think are the bravest have fearful moments. You don't have to be Fearless, just fear *less*.

Lessons Learned: Although I may not have mastered fear yet, I have discovered that I can move through it and no longer be paralyzed by it.

I truly do wish everyone could feel some of the peace I am able to attain at least some of the time - I suppose more than anything that comes from my now doing exactly what I know I should be doing. It doesn't mean I don't worry about things (money) sometimes (often) but ultimately, I have faith that something that feels this right will be supported by the universe and besides that, I have everything I need to support myself.

I am reminded of this verse I saw posted on Facebook at a time when I was getting a lot of questions as to how I do this. In my opinion, it says it all:

> *Just show up, as you are. You don't have to look or feel great. You don't have to be prepared for each challenge or know the how-to of every situation. You don't have to be fearless, or have all the answers, or be 100% ready. Nobody is all of these things. No one ever was. It's not about being perfect at all. You just have to show up as you are, despite all the objections and insecurities of your mind, despite each and every fear that threatens to hold you back, despite the limitations and criticisms others will place on you. To hell with it all. This is your life, your journey, your adventure and all it's asking of you is to show up for it, as you are. That's enough. That's more than enough. That's everything.* - Scott Stabile

Good stuff, huh? As long as you just keep showing up – and not giving up – that's enough. Sometimes it's just getting up in the morning and taking one tiny baby step toward a goal or a dream you have. Sometimes people are going to get in your way, but people will also show up to help you. Your own mind can drive you crazy, but all you can do is assure yourself that you are enough, even if you don't have all the answers at your fingertips at all times.

Be Prepared: How Much is Too Much?

I constantly hear about people trying to get their ducks in a row. But, really, who wants to be led by a line of conforming ducks? That's a little like trying to herd cats. No matter what your dream, there are things you can do to prepare, such as study and research, but don't get bogged down in too many details. You don't need to have every single detail figured out - things have a way of working out in ways you couldn't have imagined if you leave some options open. You can make endless lists on what needs to be done and possible solutions, which may or may not be a bad idea. However, that still doesn't mean you'd be prepared for anything and everything that could possibly happen (but probably won't.)

Since the time I took off in 2001, every morning I listened to my theme song and tried to move through my day "With Arms Wide Open" (by Creed). I finally accept that my life is better led by spirit than by logic - that when I let spirit and heart guide me, the way is always paved even if it appears bumpy. Even when I don't fully understand and call events that I don't agree with *negative* or *wrong* - that even then it's unfolding as it should. And God has so much more in mind for us than we do for ourselves. In our grandest dreams and our deepest wishes of what we want for ourselves - what God wants and envisions and believes us capable of - is far grander than our limited thinking can conceive of in ourselves.

Therefore, I have no problem with not knowing exactly what my next step will be - or for how long. It just doesn't need to be decided all at once - just trust that what is out there will be what you make of it - that is all the control you need...not every detail planned out...I trust - and God trusts me - that's all I need. And with surrender to this principle comes peace.

One of my first destinations when I took off was Unity Village in Missouri. I wanted to see the tower where there is always someone praying for those who have requested prayers and for the earth in general. They also have this amazing labyrinth that I wanted to walk through. As I did, I contemplated that things are never as bad as they could have been and that everything that happens or is presented to us in life is simply an experience. It is the reason we are here to begin with, to experience all that life has to offer. There really are no problems - only opportunities to experience who we are in relation to any given situation - whether we deem it a problem or a blessing, it matters not. Our only job is to experience it, learn from it, discover and decide who we are now that we've had the experience and move on.

Lessons Learned: There is a difference between being totally *fearless* and having *less fear*. I have definitely learned to Fear Less, at least enough to continue moving forward when I feel the fear - instead of letting it completely paralyze me.

The fact is - I have managed to follow my *crazy* dreams - despite being scared at times - despite not having an excess of money - despite suffering from insomnia and depression that sometimes wipes out my energy and enthusiasm for life. I've done it - maybe not in the way I imagined or would like to have it play out, not always with grace and ease or being giddy with joy - but I've pushed through and did what I wanted to do anyway.

Chapter 11

FEAR OF SEPARATION FROM LOVED ONES

One of the biggest deterrents I hear from folks thinking of following their dreams of traveling is the fear of missing their family on a daily basis. Even when their own children become adults, once grandkids enter the picture, they can often be harder to leave than their grown children.

There is no magic answer for making that part of it ache any less. Most parents feel like they want to be there for their children and help them get through life no matter how old they are. No matter how unrealistic, that's just usually included in the parent programming package.

For me, it was hardest missing the day-to-day moments that were no longer possible since I was not physically there every day. Like those moments you usually take for granted because there are so many of them. The sweet moments when the love and connection are so deep were especially hard to think of letting go. When I experienced those kinds of moments during my visits home, they were especially precious as I recognized them as a special gift.

The fact is, it's something I have struggled with from the beginning, as you can tell from what I wrote in 2003 while planning my Alaska trip:

> I've really been missing my kids lately. If anyone asks what the hardest part of traveling is, I'd have to say it's not being there for the everyday sort of things – playing mommy and being there when they're sick, missing the kisses and hugs - that's the biggest price I pay for this dream I've chosen. But sometimes passion comes with a price and for right now at least, I am willing to pay it to follow mine.

It's also a little like the cosmic tables have turned, so to speak. When I was trying to stay close to them and keep them my babies, they were wanting to grow up and be away from me. And it wasn't always easy to recognize that just because I wanted to keep them close by and safe from the big bad world, it was more important to foster a sense of independence in them. Better to encourage them to explore their own worlds and fulfill their own dreams. After all, parents aren't able to protect them from life forever.

I hope that they will now allow me that same opportunity and not begrudge their mom's journey too much. So, while it still hurts to hear my baby say she misses her mommy, I also hope that by demonstrating and proving the possibility of what some would say is impossible, that they will take that proof to their own hearts - that my granddaughter will know because she has seen it done - that she has the power to make her dreams reality. I hope that following my dream will serve a purpose, at least as helpful as my mere presence would be. Being true to myself is an example I wish to set for them.

Wakeup Call:

I was still struggling with it as shown in my journal from 2005:

In the four years that I've been on the road full-time, there have been times when I was far away from my family and wondered if the life I had chosen was fair to them. Was it right to remove myself from their lives for such long stretches of time? My daughters may both be strong and capable women with lives of their own and my teenage granddaughter is busy with all the normal (and sometimes scary) business of growing up, but that doesn't mean they won't always be my babies. I still worry about them and know that my being closer would be of help - and as a grandma, being able to spoil her only grandchild a bit more.

This dilemma was given a whole new dimension when the father of my daughters died in 2005. He had fought a particularly vicious kind of cancer for 14 years, longer than the norm for someone with multiple myeloma. Only a week after my daughter

90

first called me about his turn for the worse, he was unconscious with all doctors agreeing it was time to invoke the Directive he had signed making his wishes known for such a situation. I grabbed a flight to Austin to be with them and they didn't think he'd be alive by the time I got there.

Having someone I once loved as the father of my children and still loved as a friend, die of cancer was a real eye opener and made me look at things I'd been able to conveniently deny before then. He was only a few years older than me and even though in my teens I couldn't imagine ever living to the ripe old age of 30, now for someone to die at age 57 seemed cruel and premature.

His death was indeed a wakeup call to remind me that time could run out for anyone at any time. I remember asking myself these questions then: "Whose death do you fear the most? How about your own? Am I really okay with me dying without attempting my own dreams for my own life? Whose regrets do I prefer to deal with? Will I regret it more if I give in to what I think others need from me, or what I deny myself?"

I admit that I appreciate the sweet moments I experience getting to know myself and my own choices better. I can plan my days doing what satisfies my soul instead of waiting to see what someone else needs. It may be hard not to feel a bit guilty for such selfish thoughts, but the most important question I asked myself was, "If you're not going to start living your life for yourself now, then when?"

Caring for Parents:

Caring for aging and/or ailing parents is another big consideration that comes into play, usually about the time you're breathing a sigh of relief that you managed to survive raising your kids. There is certainly no 'one size fits all' solution here.

I have seen the many sides of the same scenario through the years as others wrestle with the same issues. I've heard the cries from daughters who are so ready to live their own lives now, as they fear their own aging, dwindling health and resources. But mom and/or dad is sick and they feel they must take care of them, or at least not move so far away from them.

You often hear the opinion or comments like, "It is not only your duty, but your privilege to take care of your parents as they get older just like they took care of you when you were young."

For many, there simply is no other choice or option, whether it's due to finances or the type of care needed. I struggled with that in my own way after the last trip my mother took with me in 2007 up the Blue Ridge Parkway. She was 81 years old then; after we got back to Austin, her health and mental state had begun to deteriorate enough that it became obvious she could no longer live alone. At first, she wanted to try assisted living since she had friends there. But it didn't take long before that was no longer an option, as she needed more intensive care after taking a fall.

I ended up staying in Austin for about three years trying to figure out what was best and no good solutions were forthcoming. All mom wanted was to go back and live in her duplex in Austin and be her old self-sufficient self again, driving other old ladies around town from church. Obviously, that was not going to happen and that was heartbreaking enough to watch my mom's eyes as she had to accept her loss of independence.

My biggest guilt came from knowing that I was failing as a suitable nurse/caregiver and could not continue on that path. Even though it had always been planned that mom would go live with my brother and sister-in-heart when that time came, it didn't lessen my guilt that I couldn't give mom what she really wanted, or at least let her stay in Austin any longer.

We often think we know what's best for those we love, whether it's little children, grown adults or aging parents. We think we can protect them better if they'd just listen and consider our ideas for them. We don't like it when they do the same to us, so we need to let it go and accept their choices.

Ideally, parents want their kids to be happy making the life for themselves that they want instead of what the parents dictate, no matter how well intentioned. Likewise, children should realize that parents are people too, with dreams and ideas of their own. And now that the job of successfully getting them to adulthood is complete, there should be no fault found in me living my own life as I choose to, no matter if anyone else understands or agrees with me.

Lessons Learned: My vow to my daughters when I held them close as newborn babies was that no matter how near or far away I was, I would do my best to protect them. But of course, I couldn't really protect them from all harm and hurt in life, no matter how much I wanted to or where I was. So why drive myself crazy with that unreachable goal? But it is possible that I can get to them and my mother within reasonable times when really needed.

Chapter 12

INHERITED FEAR
It Runs in the Family

Of course, it's common to inherit the same kinds of fear our parents and grandparents have. As children we don't have the ability to discern what is real and what is imagined; we pick up on their fear consciously or unconsciously. Therefore, you could say it runs in the family.

Financial Fears:

These fears are big and powerful and often inherited from our parents. From things I was constantly being told or denied, I always had the perception that we were basically poor folks and didn't get to do the things that folks who were better off did. As we age, these fears are then compounded by our own choices. They become even more complex when issues beyond our control happen, such as medical bills or job loss.

If you are one of those in the top three percent or so of the population with no money worries, then you probably will not be able to relate to this. For most of us, at some point, it is at least one of our worries in trying to make our dreams come true, whether it involves travel or not.

I for one, have certainly used that as an excuse for not following my dream for a lot of my life. While I believe the old adage that money can't buy happiness is true, I also agree with my mom who always said, "I don't need to be filthy rich - but I wouldn't mind getting a little dirty!"

As previously stated, I grew up with the belief that money was always in short supply. But I also grew up understanding the importance of being at least somewhat financially responsible and inherently understood how critical good credit is in getting at least some of the things you want in life.

I've heard some smug people in RV groups say that if you can't pay cash for your RV and have enough in your secure retirement fund to last the rest of your life, you shouldn't be full-time RVing. Good for them, but if I had made even half of that expectation my criteria, I'd never have even left Austin or tried to follow my dream, let alone accomplish what I have.

I did have enough for the down payment and since my plan to take temp jobs as I traveled around seemed totally workable, the trade of the security of a stable job for the freedom of adventure seemed well spent. Of course, there were times when I was scared about not having a nest egg. I did sometimes find it hard to live with the level of insecurity involved in traveling around the country without a fixed home base.

I then had to ask myself just where does my sense of security come from? Would I feel secure enough if I had enough money to live and travel on without so much anxiety? As much as I've said I'd like to have it proven to my own satisfaction, I know that it's not money alone that would truly make me happy. This has been proven to me by people I know who have more money than I'd know what to do with and are still absolutely miserable and insecure. If nothing else, they're consumed with how to keep what they have, being fearful it will be taken from them.

When people ask me even today, how I budgeted and how much I had in reserve, etc., I say that even though I'm normally a list maker and spreadsheet preparer, I just knew that if I put it all down on paper that way, the verdict would be that there was just no way it was possible. Given just the facts at that moment, that was true. But at the time I hadn't factored in the future *little miracles*, such as opportunities, chance meetings that resulted in jobs, etc. I finally got to a point that I was willing to exercise my faith a bit and not have to have every dollar accounted for in advance. My good credit got me good financing terms and I figured as long as I could find jobs, I could manage to make the payments somehow.

95

That is how it has worked for me. I ended up with a much newer and more expensive RV than I ever conceived of initially, partly because financing terms are so much better on newer units. My beautiful motorhome makes me look like I have more money than I do, so appearances can certainly be deceiving.

If you want more info in that regard, though, there are folks out there who share their budget and what it took for them to full-time in great detail. Howard and Linda Payne with RVDreams.com share budgets and expenses as they travel with their good sized 5th wheel, then motorhome. Becky Schade at InterstellarOrchard.com writes incredibly insightful and interesting articles about her life, along with financial info about what it takes for a solo female in a little Casita who boondocks a lot.

Lessons Learned: Finances are for sure, another category where one size does not fit all. There are so many factors to consider that make what works for one person totally undoable for another. Prioritize your own preferences and don't try to keep up with the Joneses.

What I Learned from Mom:

I introduced you to my mother in the chapter, *How I Began to Fear Less.* Obviously, her initial reaction to my dream was not in the least bit positive. I loved how she said she came around because, "God had a talk with her." However, I think what really sealed the deal was her being able to come on some trips with me. She later confessed that travel had always been a secret dream of hers too, but she never had the faith or hope that she could do anything about it.

I got my love of trees from my mom, an original tree hugger. Being able to share the redwoods and sequoias with her was truly a dream come true for both of us. Once when we were staying in a park that bordered a patch of huge redwoods, I woke up one morning and stepped outside of the RV to find her still in her nightgown, looking up at the tops of the trees, simply enraptured with sheer bliss all over her face. I asked what she was doing and she said, "I'm thanking God that I get to see this." She thanked me too, over and over again so often during our travels and we'd both cry in gratitude for the shared experiences.

Although she was deathly afraid of water due to a near drowning as a teenager, it was always wonderful to see her fight through those fears in the interest of exploring something new with me. When I wanted to go on a jetboat ride, she refused at first, but then changed her mind because she said I inspired her to try new things. I could actually see the nervousness in her demeanor change during the trip to one of childlike excitement. Here's what I wrote about it at the time in 2005:

> *She has always told me she wished she had the guts to do the crazy things I've done, but I am inspired by the determination she shows in being as open-minded as she is, especially at an age when most people feel perfectly justified in having an opinion and sticking with it no matter what and well past the point where it serves their highest purpose.*

What we Learned From Mickey Mouse:

When we did what I called the Grand Tour of Florida in 2002, she was 76 years old and I got the biggest kick out of how much of a little kid spirit was still left in my mom. When we walked around Disney World's Magic Kingdom, her eyes lit up like a six-year-old because we were going to eat lunch in Cinderella's Castle!

One of my favorite memories was when we were leaving a show about how the Disney cartoons are animated. We were in line behind a little girl and her daddy walking hand in hand. She looked up at him and said, "Wow, I just can't believe this!" Her dad replied, "Yes, that was great, huh?" (thinking she was referring to the show). She looked down at the pink pointed princess hat with the long sparkling scarf she got

97

from Cinderella's Castle and said, "No, I mean this..." and the look on her face as she regarded her treasure was priceless. It still brings a smile to my face when I think of the look of absolute bliss and the sound of sheer awe in her voice. I totally understood where she was coming from because I admit that I would have done anything for that kind of hat when I was that age.

I laughed out loud at mom's tears of joy when she was greeted by Mickey Mouse on the street and exclaimed as she hugged him, "Hellooo, I never thought I'd get to meet you!"

It was also outside every belief I ever had as a child that I would ever get to the Magic Kingdom. I had finally just accepted that it was out of the realm of realistic possibilities, but there I was at 51 years old with my mom finally living outside of our limited, childish vision of reality. Fun is not just for rich folks!

It really did feel like I was somehow entering a different world - a place that really had nothing to do with 'normal' reality. It was amazing that you could put yourself in a pirate's world with underground caves, then next be shooting through space on a thrilling ride in the dark with stars and planets swirling all around you, then get sopping wet plunging down a raging river, all in a day (exhausting as it may be.) It really was a 'magic kingdom.'

One of the most interesting experiences I had at Disney World was when I was gazing up at the stars on our first night there and thought how lucky I am to be able to do what I'm doing. The next loving voice I heard in my head said:

> *Luck, hell! It took courage and commitment to get where you are today. It took planning as well as letting things happen and going with the flow. It took letting some things go and acquiring other things needed. Those are the things it takes to make luck and so consider yourself lucky if you must, but also give yourself some credit for the effort it took to create that luck.*

All I had to say to that was, "Thank you, God - for giving me this world of possibilities that enable me to create what I truly want in my life."

I really enjoyed hearing more of the story behind the whole Disney concept. Walt Disney was truly a visionary who persisted with his dream despite all the dire warnings of other, more practical souls. My favorite revelation of him was his reaction to Roy, his accountant brother, when Roy alarmingly told Walt that they were $3 million in debt! Walt started smiling but Roy was panic-stricken, saying, "Walt, you don't understand! We are $3 million in debt - that's not what we made - we are $3 million in debt!" Walt started dancing around exclaiming, "Whoopee, Roy - this is great - if somebody was willing to lend us that kind of money, we must really have it made!"

What a fantastic way of looking at it - and he was right on the mark. For the first time I really heard the words to his theme song from the heart: *When you wish upon a star - makes no difference who you are - when you wish upon a star, your dreams come true.* I thanked old Walt for creating the magic and helping us believe in it like he did.

♡♡♡

Mom was 78 when she joined me in Alaska and it was fun to see her literally pinch herself and when I asked what she was doing, she said she wanted to make sure she was not dreaming. I laughed and said I still have bruises on my arm from her nudging me, "Look at that - just look at that!"

I had a certain amount of fear when she would join me because sharing a small space with her could have been a real issue. But here's what I wrote about it then in 2003:

> *It's really been a blast sharing this last leg of my journey with my mother. I had worried that we'd end up wanting to kill each other at some point since we're both such independent, opinionated women, but instead we're giggling ourselves to death*

- over the stupidest stuff - especially when we're tired we start babbling and laughing so hard about it until we both have tears in our eyes over something so dim-witted that certainly no one else in the universe would get the joke. We both laugh about how unlikely it would have seemed when I was 16 that we would ever even end up friendly, much less as close as we are now. Back then she worried that I was so rebellious I would kill her with a heart attack or something - now she hates being killed by me at Skip-Bo. (Sorry, mom, I couldn't resist. Skip-Bo is a card game my mom and I played endlessly and had a fierce competition going for years).

Lessons Learned: Mom admitted that she actually admired me for the things she initially fought with me about - my adventurous spirit and attitude. She never pursued her own dreams, so by the time she felt too old to pursue something so new and different, I was able to take her along with me on some of my adventures.

What I Learned from Dad:

At age 82, my dad died just a year after I started traveling. Since we had not been very close in life, only once or twice can I ever recall having anything that could be called a meaningful conversation with him, where we shared what were really core truths about ourselves.

During my last visit with him in the hospital, I remember thinking he looked so awful and I knew that was the last time I'd see him alive. In fact, he looked me right in the eye and told me he was tired of feeling so bad and was 'ready to go.'

Obviously exhausted, he was still trying to talk to me so I wouldn't just be sitting there. He told me that travel had also been an unfulfilled dream of his. He said he was glad I was following my dreams and not to let them go no matter what anyone else said. He talked of his regrets about not being a better father and not communicating with us more. I began stroking the top of his brow and forehead and told him gently that I loved him and to stop worrying about me - to just relax, close his eyes and go to sleep. He later told my mother what a comfort that was to him and what a tremendous help I had been during that time. At his funeral, when it was my turn to go up to say my final goodbye, I stroked his head and whispered that I hoped he realized now that he had a higher perspective; that his life had not been a failure and that I would see him again later and we'd have a good laugh about it all.

Little did I know then that I would feel his answer the next year when I was in Alaska in 2003. Ironically, it was partly because of the inheritance I got from him that I could afford the big trip to Alaska. Here's what I wrote about a strange encounter then:

A Message from Heaven:

> At one pull-off, I was taking a photo when a couple pulled in and we exchanged taking each other's picture with the view. From the first time I laid eyes on the man, Gordon, I almost passed out. He looked so much like my father that it was almost more than I could do not to keep staring at him. They say everyone has a twin somewhere and today I surely met my dad's. He looked about the same age as my dad was when he died - he had the same shape face and features, the same pale coloring, the same big ears and especially the same old-aged clouded but still brilliant blue eyes.

> I just kept looking closely at him and I swear it felt just like I was looking at my dad during the last time I saw him just a few weeks before he died. It was truly a surreal experience, but then it went from weird to bizarre. I almost fainted when he said, "Young lady, I'm a lot older than you are and I'm here to tell you that you need to follow your dreams while you can and not wait until it's too late."

> Those were almost exactly the words my dad had said to me during our last discussion about my unconventional lifestyle. It

just hit me with such clarity that somehow my dad used this chance meeting with this couple to reinforce his advice to me.

I believe those that have passed over to the spiritual side can see and watch over us, so sometimes I swear I can hear his voice in my head. I like to believe he enjoyed seeing me on that and other trips. Travel is something he always talked of doing, but a dream he never managed to make come true. That was one of the dearest lessons I learned from him - if you wait too long and hold out for just the perfect conditions before doing what you want to do, sometimes your dreams just pass you by and turn into the dreaded trio: coulda, woulda, shouldas.

Lessons Learned: I don't really remember my dad ever saying he was proud of me for anything when I was growing up. Although it was a little sad to have waited so long to hear it, it was still great to have his blessing and to have seen even a little glimpse of the real man when he was being truthful and vulnerable instead of putting on the mask that we all wear sometimes, based on what role we think we have to play. No matter how we feel about them, our parents are our first role models to demonstrate how to tackle the fears that come up in life. While they may think they have our best interests in mind by steering us away from danger, the trick is to still learn to think for ourselves as adults and make our own measured choices, no matter if our dreams are understood or shared by anyone else. I inherited fears from my parents, but I like to think I also inspired them to move beyond them as best they could.

Chapter 13
FEAR OF BEING ALONE

As previously mentioned, it was definitely a huge advantage that my best friend, Don, traveled alongside me in his Airstream for the first two years of my full-time RVing. To me, that was the best of all worlds - I had someone to explore with and laugh until we were giddy, but I also still had my own space and alone time when needed. I frequently hear people say they wouldn't want to travel alone because doing things by yourself is no fun without someone by your side to share it with.

Since I can certainly understand that point of view, it may seem strange to some that I've learned that I really prefer to travel alone. I'm always asked about getting lonely, but that just doesn't happen to me often. If I feel the need for company, there are always people to talk to at the campground. If I meet someone with similar interests and we want to spend the day together sharing them, that's great. Then I can come home, have my alone time and go through the pictures of a great day.

My daughter and I both laugh that we've seen the way other people do things and we like our way better. So maybe I'm just too danged selfish and set in my ways, but I pretty much give myself permission to feel however I feel in that regard.

There are Benefits to Being Alone:

You don't have to focus on the things you'll miss without someone there. Think about how freeing it is to do things just the way you want: when you get up or go to sleep, what and when you eat, how long to stay or when to go home, what music to listen to and how loud, what TV shows or movies to watch. Sing off key at the top of your lungs, fart, belch, whatever and you don't feel self-conscious or crude.

When I feel like it, I can stay at home all day in my jammies, puttering around, playing on the computer or binge-watching what others may consider stupid TV shows and yet, never get bored.

I hear married women complain about getting those, "I'm bored and get me outta here," looks from hubby if they want to browse around the little shops in town. As I go in and out to my heart's content, I giggle at the impatient sighs I hear from them waiting for their wives tapping their feet at the door.

As far as relationships go, I've had both the good and bad kind. But no matter how good it was, I can't imagine living with anyone in such a small space as an RV. I tried that briefly and quickly discovered that it is not for me. I know plenty of them and I am in awe of couples who can live happily together in such a confined space, but I need more privacy than that allows. I also laugh and say it's because I'm so ornery that nobody could put up with me. That may be funny, but there's a lot of truth in it too.

It may be that I haven't learned how to be in love and compromise with my partner without feeling like I have to give up too much of what is inherently me in the process. I tend to say I'm okay, when inside I am really not. Or I spout off without thinking things through, so obviously I haven't learned the fine balance between being kindly honest and too direct.

Thankfully, the RV community is friendly and helpful and gives a feeling of companionship and 'being in this together.' That is one of the coolest things about RVing - people who are living the lifestyle they choose and love; they tend to be more generous and giving and want to share it whenever possible.

For those who either choose to or have to travel alone, there are clubs and other opportunities for group camping trips or other meet-ups. *Escapees* has a solo group segment within the club and there are also specialty groups like *Loners on Wheels* and *Wandering Individuals Network*. The purpose is not to be a romantic matchmaking club, but they have frequent get-togethers and opportunities to meet others with similar hitch-itch syndrome. There are also *women only* groups like *RVing Women*, *Sisters on the Fly* and I'm sure Google could find many more.

Although I really do enjoy the times I've been able to meet up with others and make new friends, I'm personally not much of a *joiner* and it rarely works out that I'm in an area at a time when something is going on with them. I don't think I'd like the caravan concept with a group because I resist being on a fixed schedule and prefer to do things when and for how long I feel like it at the moment.

Oh, Lonesome Me:

Here are a couple of short articles I've done about lonesome roads:

An article for RVTravel.com: "Don't You Ever Get Lonely?"

> That's usually the second question I get asked after people find out I'm a single woman full-time RVer. The first is, "What gave you the idea to do something like that?" I can answer both questions with one scenario. Picture being beside the death bed of someone you love and finding out they are full of regrets, wanting just one more day to do some of the things that their heart has always dreamed of doing but had always postponed. They are leaving this life alone with many wishes unfulfilled. How lonely is that? Solitude is completely distinct from loneliness. The times when I am unaccompanied is often when I feel the most connected to everyone and everything around me.
>
> On one beautiful autumn day, I was at a park taking pictures of a blue lake and orange trees. The ground beneath me felt soft, spongy and alive. The falling leaves were vibrating and the rustling of the bird feathers were in perfect sync with the beating of my heart. I was experiencing solitude but with such a connection to everything around me; there's no way that could be

described as being lonely. In solitude you can see how much alike we are. But I have felt lonely in a room full of people.

I say share your dreams with another when you can, but don't let the fear of being alone stop you from living them.

From an article I did for the Winnebago magazine Traveling Times in 2007:

"A Woman and Her Winnebago"

Most people had one of two reactions when I said I was going to become an RVer on my own: either that I was really crazy or really inspirational. Now, after more than five years, I am often thankful that the irrational won out over the practical, because I love this lifestyle more than I can adequately express.

Some of these notes may be a repeat stated in different ways, but the message is so important. As I said, even though I'd never driven anything larger than a van before, as a woman traveling alone, I knew I'd feel more secure in a fully self-contained motor home. When parked for the night, if I ever felt threatened in any way, I could drive off pretty quickly without going outside. Learning to drive something 36 feet long (and towing a car behind it) was easier than I thought it would be and I'm glad I didn't let my fear keep me from that choice.

And the benefits - unbelievable! At times I've shared the view from my humongous windshield with my mom as we toured Alaska. We overnighted next to glacial streams and watched eagles fly overhead. We double-hugged trees in the redwoods, watched the earth boil up and spill over in Yellowstone and we both cried with joy when she said she thought she would die without her dreams of travel coming true. When we visited Disney World in Florida (thrilling the eight-year old little girl in us by having lunch at Cinderella's Castle!) we both learned the truth of: "When you wish upon a star - makes no difference who you are - when you wish upon a star, your dreams come true." It makes me happy to be able to help make her dreams come true. I've gazed in awe at the Grand Canyon, celebrated the Sunset festival in Key West and seen a lot on both coasts but I still don't feel that I've even seriously begun to explore yet. But I am content with the start I've made – at least I've started.

Driving on interstates or country roads - no matter what the scenery, there is something inherently satisfying about being somewhere I've never been before. Pulling into parks, getting all hooked up again, greeting and swapping stories with the other campers, spending a couple of days (or months) and then taking off down the road to do it all again someplace else; it often hits me in the heart how much I enjoy this lifestyle. How great to be able to make up your mind to stay or go as you please and no matter what, your comfortable home is always right there with you to bring you comfort of another sort!

So, what have I learned about solo RVing in five years? For one, that I haven't experienced all the bad things so many were sure would happen to me being on the road alone. I'm not at all careless, but I've boondocked at discount store parking lots and along scenic roadsides in Alaska and never once felt threatened. What I have come across are extremely friendly people in the RV community, campground owners and park rangers willing to go out of their way to help. I feel like I have the best of both worlds - companionship when I want it and privacy and alone time when I need it.

Am I happy with my solo RV lifestyle? You bet! What do I have to say to others who say it's too hard for a woman to travel alone? A quote I read comes to mind:

> *Start by doing what's necessary, then do what's possible and suddenly you are doing the impossible.*

Dangers in Being Alone:

No one has ever left on a trip without being told to be careful. Warnings to be wary of strangers are common, like there is the proverbial ax murderer waiting behind every bush.

I've often said I've never felt threatened in that way in all the years I've been traveling. I do not choose to live my life in paranoia, always expecting the worst from people. But I do listen to my gut and check in with it. I use what common

107

sense I have and if something doesn't feel right in any way, I hightail it out of there.

There are many differing opinions about whether you should carry a gun or other weapons so that you're ready to defend yourself at the drop of a hat. In that regard, I say everyone needs to follow their own conscience.

I've seen many suggestions of what to do to make yourself less vulnerable in this regard. Some say they put a pair of large men's boots outside the door, or a big bowl of water with *Killer* on it or something indicating you have a big, bad dog.

Something I always do is make sure I know exactly where I am when I am traveling and stopped for the night. I have the full address or GPS coordinates noted on paper kept next to my bed. If I have an emergency and must call 911, I don't want to fumble for these details when time is critical in getting help to me. I have a panic button on my key chain that makes a super loud alarm noise if I push it. I make sure I know where my car keys are at all times and if I need to, I can push the panic button on it, too. I carry bear spray when I hike, although I've heard others say wasp spray is a good deterrent, as well.

Having a dog that barks out warnings is common, of course. Since I didn't grow up with dogs, I don't know if the rewards of having one as a companion or for safety is worth it to me. When I weigh the expense and responsibility of traveling with a pet, it always comes down to me feeling I'm better off without one. I am certain there are many out there who don't agree with me on that one! But that is what I feel applies to me.

I know that taking a self-defense course is always a good idea and one of those things I keep saying I need to do and wish I had done a long time ago. So, in this regard, do as I say, not as I do and sign up for one.

Security is an Illusion:

I think it is human nature to crave a feeling of security and being safe. But in reality, no matter how much we chase it, there really is no such thing. This is one of my favorite quotes on the matter:

> *Despite our wish that the center of our lives will hold firm, it never does. Life is like an ever-shifting kaleidoscope - a slight change, and all patterns alter. One moment life feels full and perfect, and the next an accident happens or we fall sick. Settled comfortably into being single, we meet someone and fall deeply in love. We go along in one direction when an unforeseen obstacle appears and we have to swerve. Suddenly, stunningly, we are in a different life.* - Sharon Saltsberger

Another favorite on the subject:

> *Security is mostly a superstition. It does not exist in nature, nor do the children of men as a whole experience it. God himself is not secure, having given man dominion over his works! Avoiding danger is no safer in the long run than outright exposure. The fearful are caught as often as the bold. Faith alone defends. Life is either a daring adventure or nothing. To keep our faces toward change and behave like free spirits in the presence of fate is strength undefeatable.* Helen Keller

It's all about perspective. It reminds me of when my nephew, Kevin, was traveling across country on his motorcycle. He stopped by to see me and I asked him if he wasn't afraid he might get lost. I'll never forget his response, "You can't get lost if you don't care where you are. I'm just exploring whatever comes my way, so it's all good."

Lessons Learned: I'm only as alone as I want to be. How I feel about it is a choice and I can choose to focus on the positives and move forward in life instead of hiding inside waiting for someone to go out with. The point is, whether you enjoy life with or without someone, get out and enjoy it! As for security, I still say I travel with miracles and angels following me and that most people are basically kind and helpful if you give them a chance to be.

Chapter 14
FEAR OF HEALTH AND AGING ISSUES

When I started my adventure in June 2001, I was 50 years old. I had no chronic conditions that I was aware of and my energy level was good. I hardly ever had a cold, so I thought there was no better time than the present to chance this lifestyle. Like most people, I figured it was likely that I could eventually expect health issues as I aged, so there was no benefit in waiting. I wanted to be as active as I could be for as long as possible. One of the biggest attractions about travel for me was getting out in nature, hiking and enjoying the views.

I wasn't terribly afraid at that point about not having health insurance. There was no way I could handle that cost and still stay on the road, so it was a conscious decision and one I thought I could handle.

However, there were times when I was afraid of the consequences of that decision. While nothing major, I've certainly had my health concerns while traveling. The worst bout started in 2005 with a literal pain in my neck that started moving down my left arm and when my little finger was numb more often than not, I knew it was time to find out what the deal was. A member of one of my RV groups highly recommended a nearby chiropractor.

This led to an August 2005 journal entry I called, "My Degenerate Neck"

> *He took x-rays to see what was going on and how best to treat me. I almost slapped him when he said I had the neck of an 80-year-old! I thought he was rude making fun of my multiplying chins or something, but then he explained it was my discs that were degenerating. Then he had the nerve to add the*

word 'arthritis' to the mix -- now I was really not amused! I can handle being called degenerate, but I don't appreciate my body parts getting worn and arthritic before their time. And then to hear that his recommended extensive course of treatment would cost more than I could conceivably pay - the least I can say is the timing sucked big time.

I broke down and cried on his examination table as my mind immediately went to the worst-case scenario. I was able to get out between sobs: "If I were to do what you recommend, I'd have to give up traveling, go back to Austin, sell the motor home and get a job again in lawyer-land with insurance to pay for all this treatment."

And my first from-the-soul response to that scenario was, "No way - NO WAY am I ready to quit traveling - I guess I'll have to learn to live with a pain in the neck!"

I've often said that I'm not afraid of the other side of death - I just want to live my life to the fullest first. Even if I sometimes don't even know what that means, I know I'm not ready to quit exploring. As I write this in 2018, I realize that the pain went away after a few regular adjustments and all my other fears at that time did not manifest. If there's anything the thought of death brings to the forefront of our minds, it is that it makes us consider what we find valuable in life and what makes it worth living to us.

It was around this time that I first saw this letter, said to be written by an elderly woman knowing she was dying of cancer and how that changed her priorities:

I'm reading more and dusting less. I'm sitting in the yard and admiring the view without fussing about the weeds in the garden.

I'm spending more time with my family and friends and less time working.

Whenever possible, life should be a pattern of experiences to savor, not to endure. I'm trying to recognize these moments now and cherish them.

I'm not 'saving' anything; we use our good china and crystal for every special event such as losing a pound, getting the sink unstopped, or the first Amaryllis blossom.

I'm not saving my good perfume for special parties but wearing it for clerks in the hardware store and tellers at the bank. 'Someday' and 'one of these days' are losing their grip on my vocabulary. If it's worth seeing or hearing or doing, I want to see and hear and do it now.

I'm not sure what others would've done had they known they wouldn't be here for the tomorrow that we all take for granted. I think they would have called family members and a few close friends. They might have called a few former friends to apologize and mend fences for past squabbles. I like to think they would have gone out for a Chinese dinner or for whatever their favorite food was. I'm guessing; I'll never know.

I'm trying very hard not to put off, hold back, or save anything that would add laughter and luster to our lives. And every morning when I open my eyes, I tell myself that it is special. Every day, every minute, every breath truly is a gift from God. I don't believe in Miracles. I rely on them. Life may not be the party we hoped for, but while we are here we might as well dance.
- Author Unknown

So, I made the decision to carry on and count on other miracles coming my way. God knows I've had enough of them that I should have no trouble believing in that anyway, even when my faith in myself is shaky.

I think back on those times now and realize that somehow, all those pains and health worries resolved themselves without me stopping everything else in my life to deal with them. But there were still times later on, that even when I was feeling better both physically and mentally, I would ask myself if I can still handle all this. Sometimes both the RV and my body needed repairs at the same time, totally blowing any budget I had planned. I'd ask myself if it would make more sense now to move back to Austin, sell the RV and settle back into a permanent job with insurance and stability.

It wasn't like I didn't periodically review my decision to keep living the full-time RVing lifestyle. I can certainly attest to the fact that as I got older, I became more cautious about trying new things. After 10 years on the road, I remember having this debate with myself and thinking how much more I was concerned about the age of the RV and my own aging body and whether it was still safe to stay on the road.

I've heard that those concerns are normal for all of us but being normal has never been of great comfort to me. Or is it that as we age we are just more aware of the potential consequences of our decisions? We've seen too many newscasts about all the bad things that can happen and how much can go wrong? It seems to be easier to find the negatives and the deficits instead of focusing on the positive possibilities.

From my journal in 2007:

> *Regardless of what lens I look through, the fact is that I'm not getting any younger and RVing will not get easier with age. While it may be difficult at times, it is still not impossible, even for a woman going it alone at my age. I'm not the only little ole' lady out there and there are more of us all the time.*

> *When I set out at age 50, I was usually the youngest at any campground, everyone else was retired and my way of supporting myself with temp jobs was seen as very unusual. I was always jealous of those not having to work during the week and could just spend all their time doing exactly what they wanted to do.*

> *On the other hand, I also saw that many, due to their age or physical conditions, were not physically capable of doing all the more active and fun stuff I still enjoyed. It's never wise to compare yourself with others since you never know what people are really dealing with in their lives, but I find myself doing that too often anyway.*

I can't count how many stories I've heard where a couple had dreamed for years of traveling, sometimes just chomping at the bit and miserable in their present situation, but still

114

decided to wait. They'd tell themselves that just a couple more years and they'd be in better shape to give up the high paying job after saving more for a secure and worry-free retirement. And I'm sure that at times that plan does basically work out. But sometimes, there are sad tales of how one or the other fall sick or even die before they could fulfill their true dreams; that feels like a wakeup call to the rest of us.

I've been inspired by women older than me who boondock, roughing it all the time. I feel like a wuss for having a big motorhome that I prefer to have hooked up to electricity if I'm in a place longer than a few days. It's always easier to judge ourselves more harshly than we would anybody else, no matter what the comparison is about.

RVers of all Ages:

The biggest question in my mind has been answered for sure, that it is possible to do what you want to do regardless of your age. Recently, I've learned that doesn't have to mean how old you are; too young is not an excuse these days, either. It's been very interesting to watch the changing demographics for RVing since I began in 2001.

While not a fear, there was a vague discomfort about usually being the youngest at any RV gathering. Twelve years later, I was invited to a gathering where I realized I was the oldest one there. That too, brought on a vague discomfort. It's normal to want to feel accepted with a sense of belonging in any group situation, but there is something to be gained in what you learn about yourself and the world you live in, no matter what the age of the group.

A few years ago, after following them online, I met a young couple, Chris Dunphy & Cherie Ve Ard (Technomadia), who shared info online about how they carved out a successful traveling lifestyle and supported themselves along the way. Their service, *Mobile Internet Resource Center*, provides both free and subscription-based information to help other travelers wade through the confusing maze of what are the best plans and providers for internet and cell phone services. Since more jobs can be done while traveling now due to being connected in this way, this became an important and valuable niche to share, along with their knowledge and experience of older bus conversions.

I happened to be back in Austin when they were there and I was happy to be invited to a get together with other RVers whom they hosted. It's always cool to meet people in person that you have become familiar with for years online. It was here that I met another young couple, Heath & Alyssa Padgett. Newly married, they came up with the idea of traveling and working a job in every one of the 50 states. They've gotten sponsors since then and have not only made a success of their own life on the road, they now have this great resource, *The RV Entrepreneur*, where they share what they've learned with others via podcasts, video and written material.

Another couple, Travis and Melanie Carr, are related to the originators of the Escapees RV Club, Kay and Joe Peterson, who started it in 1978. When I first started researching full-time RVing, Escapees was a unique resource and service. Since these were the days before social media, their forum was the best place to relate to others who were going through the process of wanting to learn and experienced RVers willing to share their knowledge. As the club has grown and demographics changed, Travis and Melanie founded the younger version of the club, Xscapers, for those still working full-time while traveling and even raising families on the road.

As we introduced ourselves around the campfire, I said that it did feel kind of weird to be the old timer of a group. I don't know if they could even relate to what I was talking about - how I first had to access the internet when I took off in 2001. After waiting in line at a campground to get to the landline phone connection and then waiting for that distinct AOL dialup tone, you could still never take for granted that you could get online. That was before Facebook and social media made it so easy to keep in touch with family and friends and Google made research a breeze.

But we were all connected by our mutual love of travel, so by the time we parted company, I was thrilled to have made these new friends and greatly admire their adventurous spirits. I've met quite a few families on the road who are homeschooling their older children, but I have another kind of respect for those having babies and making that all work in such a small space.

It's cool that we all have a lot to learn from each other, no matter the age. It's also a cool perk of life, no matter what the lifestyle, to be able to share something helpful with someone who wants to do the same thing you're doing. They often feel they lack whatever it is to make it actually happen for themselves. By your example, showing they CAN do what you're doing is not only comforting but encouraging.

It seems that no matter what your age, health condition or disability, there is a club or group to inspire you to follow your dream with people who have been there and done that; you won't have to feel your fears are unique and unbeatable. There is virtually nothing these days except death that can stop you and since that comes all too quickly, you might as well get the most out of life while you can.

And speaking of death, because old historical cemeteries are some of my favorite day trips, I'm frequently reminded there of how short and fragile life can be when I visit them. I wrote about this experience in 2005 when I was walking around old Jacksonville Cemetery in Oregon:

> *I walk around in the still quiet, wondering about what these people's lives were like - how they lived, how young they died - what made them leave the security of what was known about the world at that time to journey into uncharted and dangerous territory. These guys were the pioneers who blazed the roads that RVers ride on so comfortably today.*

When I was getting ready to leave, I had an encounter where this big rabbit stood and looked directly at me for a strangely long time before hopping off. Later that night I remembered an old Native American legend, a story about a rabbit and fear:

117

A long time ago - no one really knows how long ago it was - Rabbit was a brave and fearless warrior. Rabbit was befriended by Eye Walker, a witch. The witch and Rabbit spent much time together talking and sharing - the two were very close. One day as they were walking, Rabbit said, "I'm thirsty." Eye Walker picked up a leaf, blew on it and then handed Rabbit a gourd of water. Rabbit drank but didn't say anything. When Rabbit said, "I'm hungry," Eye Walker picked up a stone and changed it into a turnip. Rabbit ate with relish but still didn't say anything. When Rabbit tripped and fell, she used a magic salve to heal his great pain and still he said nothing.

Several days later as Eye Walker was searching for her friend, he was nowhere to be found. When she finally met up with him by accident, she asked why he was avoiding her. He answered, "Because I am afraid of you and your magic. Leave me alone!"

She responded, "I see - I have used my magical powers on your behalf and now you turn on me and refuse my friendship." Rabbit did not even see the tears in Eye Walker's eyes. He said he hoped never to see her again.

Even though Eye Walker could have killed Rabbit right then, she refrained, but cursed him with these words, "From now on, you will call your fears and your fears will come to you." Now Rabbit is the Fear Caller. He goes out and shouts, "Eagle, I am so afraid of you." If Eagle doesn't hear him, he calls louder, "Eagle, stay away from me!" Eagle, now hearing Rabbit, comes and eats him."

As this story shows, Rabbit medicine people are so afraid of tragedy, illness, disaster and being taken that they call those very fears to them to teach them lessons. The keynote here is: *what you resist will persist - what you fear most is what you will become.* In my Animal Medicine cards, it says, "If you pulled Rabbit, stop talking about horrible things happening and get rid of 'what if' in your vocabulary. This may signal a time of worry about the future or of trying to exercise control over that which is not yet in form - the future. Stop now!"

118

Lessons Learned: Concentrating only on the fearful things calls them to you. Stop focusing on them, affirming them - that only strengthens them.

Whether you're young or old, it's not wise to put off until *later*. Sometimes later never comes or you wait too long and it just passes you by because you're too busy to notice its progression.

♡♡♡

No Matter the Age, Death can Sneak Up on You:

My heart has always been saddened by the tales of some of my fellow dreamers whose lifelong plans of travel were quashed by death or jeopardized by life-threatening illness. But my spirit has been uplifted by the lessons they've imparted on not waiting because we never know what's lying in wait for us around the next bend.

I introduced you before to the group had formed out of the Escapees RV Club Forum of folks who were going to start full-time RVing in 2005. When Tab first invited me to the Quartzsite rally, I balked a bit about the advance timing. Talk about inspiration - I've frequently given thanks that I decided to go after getting to know some of the people from their posts to the group and how excited they were. I've always considered it one of my best blessings to have met this group of inspiring people in person, many of which are still dear friends today.

When I was reading the advance posts, I was particularly touched by one woman about my age (in my early 50s at the time) who had struggled for a long time to begin full-timing. She battled with her family's objections, her own guilt about leaving them and her fear about everything - from backing up her trailer to running out of money on the road. She had been preparing for at least 3 years at the time, but she was determined to be with the rest of the group at the Quartzsite, AZ big RVing lollapalooza. She in particular was always an encouraging force for others taking the steps toward their goals. I was really looking forward to meeting her.

She first posted in 2003: "Hi. I am so happy to have found this site. I am a single woman and am planning to purchase an RV and hit the road within the next year. My mother and sister are having a hissy fit because they think it is not safe for a single woman. Are there many single women on the road full-time? I'm hoping someone can share their experience with me. Also, is there anyone full-time in an RV smaller than 20 ft.? (not only am I a single woman, but I am a poor single woman)."

She experienced obstacles and delays but was planning to meet the group in Quartzsite despite her fear. Some of her posts were a mixture of sharing both encouragement and fears:

> "Will you be in Quartzsite in Jan, 2006?" she had written. "You can't miss me; I will be the woman (towing silver Avion) with the white-knuckle grip on the steering wheel and hair standing on end.

> When I think about towing the trailer I can get pretty anxious. I told a friend that I did not know where I would end up because I can only drive straight or maybe turn left. He thought I was joking and I didn't tell him any different. The thoughts of making right-hand turns make me...I'm probably really scaring everyone now.

> I'm going to get on the road this year come hell or high water, but you have no idea how scared I am. I'm not gonna let that stop me though! You call me 'courageous' but my family calls me insane.

Even when those she loved the most did not understand...

> I wish I could say that my family supports my decision to RV full-time, but they do not. My sister thinks I am weird and my mother feels like she is being abandoned. How did I overcome it? I can't say I have completely. I don't like the fact that my decision to full-time has caused my mother pain, but not long

120

ago, it dawned on me that I am 52 years old and still asking for my mother's approval on how I live my own life! Something very wrong with that.

Later: Thanks to all of you for taking time to respond. After much thought I realized that I don't care so much about people thinking I'm nuts, as much as I worry about my mother. She wants me to wait until she dies and I want to go now while I am in good health. I understand that she is fearful, but I am going to do this and I will try to make it as easy on her as possible by visiting as often as I can.

So, we were all wondering what happened and why she wasn't there. It wasn't until after the rally that we were shocked to hear that she had passed away unexpectedly, shortly before the rally. Kathy Wells' (Silver-Twinkie) inspiring posts were included in the Full-time Class of 2005 Yearbook I later did for the group and I know that she was with us in spirit.

This was part of the notice to the group:

This is Kathy's sister (Lavada). I just got into her email file and thought I would let you know that Kathy passed on January 2, 2006. She died a peaceful death and I was so fortunate to be able to spend the last 5 months with my 'lil sis. She was the most intelligent, creative person I've known. It was so hard giving her up. All she wanted was to get in her RV and travel and never got the opportunity.

Another comment: Kathy would want me to tell you all to accept her passing as she did and to learn from it that *one should never put off a dream if it can be made possible today!*

Kathy, your classmates will raise a glass to your memory at every rally around the campfire from now on and will carry you in our hearts down the road. Godspeed to you, our friend. ♡

The following quote was also one of her mottos:

Life is not a journey to the grave with the intention of arriving safely in a pretty and well-preserved body, but rather sliding in broadside, thoroughly used up, totally worn out and proclaiming, "Wow, what a ride!"

- Unknown author, but used by many spiritual teachers

Lessons Learned: Kathy persisted with her dreams despite all the objections from everyone around her who thought they knew what was best for her. But none of them knew that despite her persistence, her dreams could not come true. Life took another direction and ended for her before then. But the fact that she kept working toward her goal is inspiring and we all should learn from her experience and not sit back complacently waiting for those dang ducks to line up!

Chapter 15
FEAR OF ANXIETY AND DEPRESSION

Why is an article on depression included here when the intent is to offer positive and inspiring suggestions? Because depression and anxiety are my own biggest fears. I know that they are also major fears for many throughout their lives. It's something I've dealt with before I even thought of the possibility of travel and something that returns all too often, despite the joys I've found in this lifestyle.

Because I share the beauty and benefits of what I experience in a way that makes people say they feel like they're right there with me, most people are surprised to hear of the debilitating sadness that comes over me. It often totally paralyzes both my body and spirit, leaving me anxious and discouraged.

I picture it as a massive dark cloud that as it grows denser, completely blocks the sunlight of reason and is always threatening to completely envelop me. The despair deepens and at times, I can barely breathe as getting out of bed is too much of an effort.

Since I started sharing my experiences from the very beginning, I have written publicly about my depression issues. I knew I wasn't the only one who dealt with this, but so often I heard from others saying that was a big reason they couldn't make their own dreams come true: it isn't just fear that needed to be moved past, but strong depression robs us of the simple ability to think straight. Therefore, I knew how important it was to share that too.

Good and Bad Days:

Many read about my good times and see my life as one big happy hour. Sometimes when I hear from people who say they've been inspired, it starts my day with a smile and "Thank you, God, for letting me have my dream with the bonus of showing others they can have theirs too."

Then there are other days when I read the same kind of message and think to myself, "If they only knew what a fraud I am!" I write honestly, but sometimes I think people misinterpret who I really am. Or that I have something they don't possess that allows me to live my dream; they think that until they have the exact same thing, they can't follow their heart. So - here's the truth: I am NOT always brave - I am NOT always confident or sure of what I'm doing. Sometimes I just want to crawl in a hole and die and never have to lie about being glad to be alive again.

The Dreaded Triple A's:

I once described depression as the triple A's - when you feel Alone, Abandoned and Adrift. We've all been told that when making decisions, we create the choices and judgments to go with our feelings and we need to trust our gut.

But I've come to believe that feelings are not always right. Sometimes you have to dig deeper for those things that you *naturally* know, despite how things appear in the moment. What I call 'natural knowing' are those things that are inherent truths that come from the deepest part of me; even if I can't explain them rationally, I accept them as true because to me they are just undeniable, even if not understandable to any other person.

Sometimes I even feel forgotten by God and my prayers become combinations of pleas and accusations: "Where are you, Father - how dare you abandon me at the worst possible time in my life? I used to be so aware of your presence and power in my life. I used to feel blessed and brave. Now I feel cursed and cowardly." After a while, I don't even want to get better and my most passionate prayer is just for everything to end. "Please, just fade to black for the last time and don't let me wake up." If my most honest wish had been granted at those times, I surely wouldn't be alive now to share anything with you.

In an effort to understand such powerful negative emotions, I ask myself: *Is that Who I Really Am?* I know that those feelings come from a perspective of lack, certainly not the best vantage point from which to view life.

Am I really Alone? I may feel like that when I get caught up in a web of sorrow. But what I know is that I have a support group of people, angels and God himself who love me and will never leave me alone when I choose not to be.

Am I really Abandoned? I may feel like it when things don't go the way I think they should, but what I know is that I am only abandoned if I ignore the blessings that I do have and do not call on them to assist me in times of need. As I've often heard, when God feels distant, it's you that has moved, not Him.

Am I really Adrift? I may sometimes feel that I am without purpose, but what I know is that my journey in life goes on, day-by-day, step-by-step in a meaningful way. It is constant, even when I'm not aware of it, even when I take it for granted and can't find the reasons, much less understand and acknowledge them.

Yet despite what I know, naturally or not, sometimes just the smallest thing can set me off course. I think we are given super-human strength to get through the big challenges - like the adrenaline a mother uses when she lifts a car off her trapped baby. But it's the little things that come at me like gnats and catch me off-guard that leave me reeling. I may know in my mind that it's really not that bad, but somehow, I can't stop myself from breaking into tears and calling everything into question, including my very reason for being. I call those moments my *mini meltdowns*.

When I'm even halfway in my *right* mind, I analyze it and think that depression gives me a grand excuse. It gives me permission to be a slug and do nothing and just cower under the covers and do my best to ignore the world around me and especially my own life.

Returning "Home"

I began noticing that it overtook me more often when I was back in Austin to visit family after being on the road for a while. Maybe because I was always afraid I'd get trapped there again and not be able to leave, since it was hard enough to break away the first time. In looking over past journal entries, I first wrote about this in 2002:

> *I've been slipping in and out of a space I call the dark place since I've returned to Austin - that place that's ruled by fear and conflict and where peace and security cannot reside. Don tried to make me see that what I saw as obstacles were no worse - and in fact less so - than the ones I faced when I left town almost a year ago. But by this time, I was teetering on the edge of that black pit of depression I knew all too well and which always leaves me paralyzed with indecision and the inability to just make a move - any move.*

> *I have been humbled to see that I could go from feeling so high above the clouds to feeling closed in and suffocated by swirling masses of dark thunderclouds that I could not see through. Sometimes I feel that depression is like a huge bird of prey stalking me, ready to swoop down with sharp claws outstretched and once caught, I'll at least be scratched and bloodied before escape is possible again.*

> *Out of experiences such as this, I always try to identify the 'purpose' or at least a lesson learned from the difficulty. One thing I did find out for sure is that this life is the one I want for myself. Even if it is not always easy, even if it takes everything I have, this is what I want to do. There is something so invigorating to me about the new places, people and experiences that accompany this lifestyle that there is just no doubt this is what I'm supposed to do.*

> *Even though there's a certain fear involved in just getting behind the wheel of this huge machine once it's been parked for a while,*

126

there follows an excitement and confidence, as well as pride in myself for pulling it off once again.

Quartzsite - RV Mecca:

So obviously, I went through that dark and confusing maze and came out on the other side at that time. The next time I wrote about it was a few years later as I was getting ready to meet that group of newbie full-timers in Quartzsite who said they had been inspired by my example. I don't know if it was part of the recovery from an illness I had, or I was just nervous about talking before a group or what, but here's what I wrote in January, 2006:

Then about the time I was physically able to get out of bed, I no longer wanted to. It felt like there was really no reason to - that I had nothing to look forward to. The black cloud of depression had descended. I knew my brain was not working right - my eyes weren't even focusing and my thoughts were totally skewed. It seemed every commercial on TV talked about how depression hurts everyone and how my life was waiting for me. But there was no joy in looking to the future - only dread and fear and a feeling of complete hopelessness that nothing will ever be fun and light again.

It's hard to explain what clinical depression feels like to someone who has not experienced its depths. My mom says she's gotten the blues before, but not the debilitating paralysis I felt. It seemed too much trouble to do the most basic things - brushing my teeth felt like a major accomplishment - I was exhausted and winded from doing the dishes - washing my hair felt like a wasted effort and going outside became a stressful event.

Good thing making sense was never a big draw to me - after some thought, being happy seemed a much better goal to work toward. Pictures of the places I've been blessed to see flashed across my monitor as my screen saver and I am sometimes amazed at all the incredible places I have been - I remember clearly how tears of joy flowed as I sat alongside the melting Kluane Lake on the way to Alaska, just from the sheer beauty of the experience or stood and watched the earth bubble and boil at Yellowstone. Having bears in my backyard in Alaska and buffalo cross in front of my windshield in Yellowstone - what do I really need to have that would be worth trading those kinds of experiences for? How long before I would be full of regret for living my life based on the fear of what could happen instead of the faith in the good that could come? One of the things I read that got through to me was said by Helen Keller:

> *When one door of happiness closes, another opens;*
> *but often we look so long at the closed door*
> *that we do not see the one*
> *which has been opened for us.*

When I finally got to Quartzsite, I was greeted by old and new friends and that finally got me through the dark clouds. One couple exclaimed, "Malia - I can't believe we're finally meeting you - YOU'RE the reason we went to Alaska last year!" And another couple, "You're the reason my husband agreed to go to Alaska next year!" He said he read every page I wrote and figured, "If that little lady can do that all by herself, we should be able to!" It still amazes me that people are actually strongly affected by what I have done and written about.

After I wrote about how I had been feeling and that I almost didn't go, I heard the most encouraging things that couldn't help but lift my spirits and at least make me think that I wasn't alone in these feelings:

From a friend I met in Seattle who was contemplating going full-time:

> *My first reaction on reading this was "Hey! Someone has finally said that full-timing is not the cure-all for all of life's experiences! It's great to hear what I always suspected the reality was, but for some reason, no one ever writes about it. I think you've got a classic here."*

I've gotta say that while full timing is not the cure-all for everything, neither is anything else. But I still haven't found a lifestyle I like better or that is more rewarding in so many ways.

I finally ended up with a renewed conviction that things really do happen for a reason and bumps in the road do not mean the end of the trail. There's a saying I have taped to my makeup mirror that I apparently haven't reviewed enough: *Always know in your heart that you are far bigger than anything that can happen to you.* Somehow, I started to believe that the things that happened to me that I judged as bad meant that somehow the universe was not on my side anymore and that some nasty power lurked out there just to get me.

I had to start listening to my own advice to the group: Don't forget why you started RVing - don't lose your adventurous spirits - don't take the wonder of travel for granted. Don't forget that even the longest journey begins with but a single step - and baby steps count.

No Magic Cures:

I haven't discovered any magic answers or treatments for depression, so I'm sorry I can't share any cures here. I won't get into all the meds and treatments I've had for depression but suffice it to say nothing worked for long and the side effects can be worse than the condition, so I choose to just deal with it as it comes along and ride the wave through it. But I have learned that it comes and thankfully, goes.

And the most useful and wise quote that I have ever heard that applies to this and actually everything else in life, both good times and bad, is "This too shall pass."

Sometimes I think these dark times come for reasons that we can't comprehend in the moment. Perhaps it can simply be to rise above them and never give up.

Even when I find help hard to recognize, much less accept, I realize it's the support and encouragement of family and friends that keep me going. I know this to be true for sure: *I believe that friends are quiet angels who lift us to our feet when our wings have trouble remembering how to fly.*

These angels help me remember that all progress is not lost when I stumble. And there is always a second chance. A friend sent this poem to me a while back entitled:

Start Over

When you've prayed to God so you'll know his will
When you've prayed and prayed and you don't know still
When you want to stop because you've had your fill...
Start over.

When you think you're finished and want to quit
When you've bottomed out in life's deepest pit
When you've tried and tried to get out of it...
Start over.

When the year has been long and successes few
When December comes and you're feeling blue
God gives a January just for you...
Start over.

I am thunderstruck at how blessed I am and how often I forget that. A certain amount of fear and insecurity in any endeavor is a good thing because it keeps us on our toes. When I have a bit of a panic attack I tend to get upset with myself. After all the proof I've been given, it seems unforgivable to keep questioning and doubting. I got up one morning when I didn't have a job to go to that day and asked God if it was OK that I was so scared. I then heard his answer very clearly through my heart: "Of course it's okay - in fact it's even necessary. If you were 100 percent sure and had every detail lined up and all the money you needed to begin with, then this journey would not be so inspiring - not for you and not for anyone else who heard about it or encountered you during it. And while it's ok to be concerned and take whatever steps are necessary to make the money you need, you can also trust that you will be taken care of and your needs will be met. You have all the talent and resources you will ever need and I will be there with you - you cannot fail."

Growth can be painful and challenging sometimes, but ultimately if we don't do it, we die in one way or another. If we sit idly by while our dreams die, the mourning will be immense once we realize what our neglect has cost us. Was it the job of your dreams, the love of your life, your great chance to actually be what you want to be?

This journey is crammed with growth - and maybe sometimes I am afraid and have my share of doubts. But I vow to never stop testing my wings. If given the choice, I choose adventure over complacency. As reminded by a great book I read, *Listen to the Drum*, by Blackwolf Jones:

> *Where there is fear, there is a master.*
> *Either you will master fear or fear will master you.*
> *But there will be a master.*

♡♡♡

Snippets from My Conversations with God about Depression :

1.   God is talking to me all the time, but am I listening?

Be aware of what you're hearing - don't dismiss it as coincidence. Act fearlessly and immediately on what you hear. Don't wait because your mind will talk you out of what your soul desperately wants.

2.   My thoughts are sometimes dark, depressing and hopeless and I haven't been able to stop these thoughts. How can I change this when these are my real feelings? Is *fake it till you feel it* enough?

Making any effort is better than wallowing in the feeling of helplessness. No progress can be made from there.

3.   Why do I feel like it may be preferable to die rather than to continue living at this point?

Because you are afraid of your life - you are letting fear rule your feelings.

4.   How do I change that, please?

Baby steps, remember - one thought at a time - catch yourself and try to find a more positive spin to it. It doesn't have to be as dark as you portray your future to be and your present is not as bad as you make it. I am with you all the time.

Obviously, the Universe conspires to help us!

Lessons Learned: Life is all about change and progress, not staying the same or going backwards. Understanding that this process is good and necessary for our growth is just part of the lessons we learn in life: going forward even when we want to go back.

Wherever I am, is where I want to be is an important lesson I learned from Don. I recently read a similar lesson expressed by a wise man: *Contentment is being happy with what is.* I may have a long way to go before I accept that sacred truth, but I'm working on it.

And, when given the choice, I choose to be happy…so help me God.

Chapter 16
FEAR OF DEATH
New challenges

At the end of July 2018, after just starting my long planned for summer in Colorado, I was diagnosed with Stage 4 lung cancer. Throughout all the stages of denial, feeling every emotion imaginable, I got through all the tests, along with an unbelievable amount of aggravating doctor visits. I was told that it is terminal, with an average life expectancy of a year. I finally sat down to ponder how I might share this. I knew I wanted to get my experiences down in writing for my own clarity if nothing else. Not only will the process help me understand and sort out my own varying emotions, but on the chance that it might be of help to others, I'm willing to share.

When I first began to accept the diagnosis, I had the thought, "Well, at least I know now what the last chapter of this book will be." The title *Fear of Death* jumped across my mind and I had to giggle with the angels on that one. I stopped laughing when I realized that in order to explain why I had no fear of death, I'd have to speak about the experience I relate below that I have rarely shared with anyone in all these years. Why? Usual reasons like: people will think I'm crazy, nobody will believe me, I'll be written off as some New Age druggy, lunatic, etc. Then again, nothing about this had anything to do with my original intent in sharing my journey. Yet, as always, life has a way of throwing curve balls that find us no matter how we duck and swerve. So, I sucked it up and included my out of body experience here because it turns out the whole Fear Less theme wouldn't make much sense at this point without it.

Since I've shared the diagnosis with family and friends, I've heard how brave I am and how well I'm handling this. The truth is I'm just expressing how I really feel. I go through different emotions, but the fact of the matter is I think that I come across as brave because in the deepest part of me, I feel that that this is my right time to pass on. I believe that's the reason for the peace I feel about the timing now, but it started with the incident I'm going to relate now.

The following story is of an experience that happened long ago but has had a lasting impact on my entire life and how I feel about it. I came out of it with no fear of death since I believe I know what awaits me on the other side. Even now, I would be lying if I said I didn't fear some things about the process of dying because, like every other human being, I certainly want to avoid being in lingering pain if I can help it. Toward that end, I am grateful to now live in Oregon where the Right to Die with Dignity is granted to those like me so that fear of the *dying process* is at least partially allayed because it gives me some control over it.

This unusual experience happened when I was 21 years old and I had no clue what had really gone on. At that time, I had never heard of an out-of-body experience nor a near-death experience. Somehow, I knew that something important had happened, but I struggled with how to put things into words so that they wouldn't sound too weird. I keep wanting to find a way to explain this experience in a way that makes sense. Honestly, it takes more time to explain what happened than the time that elapsed in the actual experience.

It occurred not long after I moved to Austin from New Orleans in 1971. I specifically remembered it was the day of a Rod Stewart concert in San Antonio. Based on that information, I was able to Google it and get the exact date: July 27, 1971, exactly 47 years ago at this writing.

Held in the Arms of God:

Even though my memory may sometimes falter, there are details I vividly remember about this experience that seem weird even to me. There are other things I can't remember; I don't know why that is but will relate as much of it as possible, even if it still doesn't make sense to me after all this time.

A girlfriend and I were waiting in my apartment for a friend of hers to give us a ride to the concert. But before he got there, I had developed a horrible headache. They had always been incredibly rare for me, but it quickly became serious enough for me to second guess the wisdom of going to listen to loud music that day (another rare thing for me.)

When her friend arrived, I noted that he was quite handsome with long brown hair and beautiful brown eyes. His name was James. I knew my friend had a huge crush on him and I remember thinking that maybe it would be a good idea to let them go without me. When I told them that the headache was making me think I should just stay home, James suggested that he could get rid of it for me with no pills or drugs of any kind. He said if I would lay down and close my eyes, he would do *energy work* on me using his hands, but not actually touching my body, and the headache would be gone.

I remember thinking that sounded kind of crazy and unbelievable, but I'd done crazier things in my life, so why not? I remember walking through the beaded curtains into my bedroom and he instructed me to lay down on my waterbed. (Hey, it was the 70s remember and I was certainly a hippie chick.) I also feel compelled to say here, that even though I'd been a pot smoker, I had never done any heavier drugs. Neither my friend or I even had any pot at that point. Therefore, I wasn't stoned in the least and hadn't even taken an aspirin. So, in any case, this was not a drug-induced experience in any way.

Here are the things etched in my memory:

After I laid down with eyes closed, I could feel his hands moving around my head and shoulders, but he wasn't actually touching me. At some point, I could feel energy coming from the top of my head. It felt like something was being drawn out through a funnel and the next thing I knew, I was up in the corner of the room looking down on James and my body. I could see him softly moving and waving his hands around my body without touching me in any way. Then I saw him get up and go wash his hands. I remember a feeling of deep awe, as I realized that it really was my body down there and thought, "Wow, nothing that is important about me has anything to do with that body." It wasn't that I was repulsed by it or anything like that, but I understood that I was really in spirit and that was my true being, not that *vehicle* down there on the bed.

I remember understanding that the spot on the top of my head where I left my body was a *valid exit/entry point* (which correlates to the soft spot on a baby's head after birth.)

I remember being aware that I was in the corner of the ceiling, but when I glanced up, I could see that there was no solid ceiling there. All I could see was this huge galaxy with what I thought were sparkling stars. The thought began in my mind, "Wow, all I have to do is think it and I'll be up there." And before the thought was complete, I found myself traveling through those stars like you see in Star Trek, but it wasn't dizzying or disorienting in any way.

As I moved through them, I saw that the stars were actual living beings of light. There was an infinite number of them and then I understood these were beings who loved and had a real interest in me. I could feel the pure love and good wishes for me as I moved through them. I remember being amazed that there were so many of them; I felt I knew them and I wanted to stop and talk to each one of them because they would all have been joyous reunions.

However, the next thing that happened made me not want to ever experience anything or be anywhere else except right there.

I became aware of being surrounded by a pure white light that was more brilliant than I could ever possibly describe in this lifetime. I remember thinking that if I had earth eyes, it would probably blind me but now all it felt was amazingly comforting.

I felt a slight pulsation and then realized I was being gently held within that light. I felt like a baby being rocked in the strong arms of an extremely loving father. I knew I was always safe here without being told anything at all. As I even started the question in my mind about where I was and what was happening, I intuitively and without a doubt understood that I was being held in the arms of God and he loved me more than I could possibly comprehend. When people talk about Unconditional Love on this earth, it is a pale description of what God's love is really like.

As overwhelming as that was, the questions started in my mind and before I could even finish them, I 'heard' the answers and they all made sense. Even the ones that couldn't possibly make sense to us on this earth. Like Hitler or the genocide of Native Americans, or wars or how pollution is affecting our earthly home.

I can't describe it as a formal *life review* but I was able to look back on times in my life. I could see how even the tiniest kindness toward others here are of more value than gold. And I also saw so many missed opportunities I had to make a difference in another life because I thought I was just too busy or passed it by. That was a missed opportunity for me more than for anyone else. I remember feeling disappointment in myself as I saw those times and understood that the point is not to punish yourself, but to be more aware of our actions (and inactions) and that they have consequences, even when we are not able to see them in that moment.

I understood that there is no judgment there except what we place upon ourselves. We judge ourselves (and each other) much more harshly than necessary in most cases. It is not possible for God's love to be anything but unconditional and even that is an understatement.

I understood that another important point being made was that we are all indelibly interconnected to each other and our idea of being separate beings is not at all accurate. The best way I can try to describe it is being shown a silky sheet covering what looked like heads bobbing up and down. The sheet was just one living unit, but the little heads that looked distinct were all part of it that made up just one organism. I could clearly see how a ripple from one affected the whole.

I was somewhat aware that there was a huge universe of beings and dimensions on the other side of the white light that provided all kinds of new experiences. The incomparable beauty of the feelings, scenes and music there, can't even begin to be translated into any earthly experience that we've ever had.

Oh, and as for time? I understood that everything is actually happening all at once and now is all we really have. Don't ask me to try to explain all that now, but it made total sense to me then.

Obviously, I was pretty overwhelmed but felt completely comfortable at the same time. I communicated with God as my loving father (he specifically requested calling him the more informal term, *papa*, since he wants us to feel that familiar with him). Our communication was not at all with words but simply by forming thoughts; even then, not exactly like we do here on earth, since it takes so much longer to form thoughts in the words we use. It was transmitting whole concepts all at once and the answers came the same way. I now call that kind of communication *instant downloads* because they happen in a nanosecond.

After asking probably thousands of questions, I wondered what came next or if I would ever be back in human form. Again, before the thought was complete, I felt myself being drawn away and I knew I was being sucked back in through the top of my head. I started protesting, saying I wasn't ready to go back, but the deed was already in motion. That was when I understood how powerful our thoughts are and how they immediately start actions that have consequences we don't necessarily intend.

I was not happy about leaving that loving light and I asked God on the way down if I would remember everything I had just learned here because it was so important. The response was that I would not remember all the answers to specific questions because we're just not meant to understand everything on this earth or there would be no point in being here. But what I heard just as I was being sucked back in was, "All you need to remember is this:

It is ALL Right - And All is Well."

By the time I was fully back in my body, it didn't make nearly as much sense and I was totally shocked to see James just returning from washing his hands. Therefore, the entire experience couldn't have taken but a minute or so of earth time. I knew I had just learned a lifetime's worth of truth. I never told my companions what happened, I guess out of fear of feeling silly. I just remember that my headache was gone and we left for the concert in San Antonio. I remember looking out the window at the passing scenery and felt a little disoriented because I knew there was so much more out there than I could see with my eyes or feel with limited earth senses.

It wasn't until many years later that I heard what an out-of-body experience was and I thought it came closest to what I had spontaneously experienced. Something about whatever energy James had in his hands maybe drew my spirit out of the top of my head while all he was trying to do was get rid of my headache.

Since then, I have read and researched as much as I could about it and have even tried everything I could to repeat that experience with absolutely no success. I had an overwhelming desire to go back and be held in God's arms again. More than anything, I wanted everything to make sense again.

I sometimes still get flashes of insight or hear things that I instinctively know is truth and I call those things *natural knowing*. I don't have to understand or justify how they're true, I just know they are and have learned not to question them.

They're usually accompanied by deep emotion welling up, like happy tears.

I loved the clarity of the answers and understood a whole lot more about this life on earth than I feel like I do now. I don't understand why I still walk around feeling so blind and dumb about the true nature of things after an experience like that. I don't know exactly what happens right after death or about reincarnation. I also know that I'm not afraid of it and that once I am free of this Earth again, I will remember that *it is ALL right and all is well.*

The biggest take away in all this is that I have had no fear of death since then.

Accepting the fact that my earthly life will end soon, I'm thankful for the life I've had, but also am a bit relieved that many of the things I feared about growing old, I don't have to worry about now at all. Since I've never had an abundance of savings, money was always a concern. My fear was that I'd end up a penniless old lady. There is a definite gift in that life-long worry being removed.

I'm trying to adjust to this new way of life no matter how long it lasts. But it surely isn't easy going from an energetic on the road traveler to someone who just wants to be in bed most of the time. How do I feel about knowing that I will be dying soon? Maybe I could have done more with my life, but I did a lot. Maybe I could have seen more, but I've seen more than most people do in a lifetime.

I don't feel cheated or that I'm dying too soon. I can't help but feel grateful that I have had all these years of travel while I was young enough to do the serious hiking and other activities that I couldn't begin to do now. If I had waited until traditional retirement age, I'd have only been traveling now for about two years and that would not be nearly enough! I'm sure I'd feel like I had missed out and be angry at myself for waiting.

Lessons Learned: Don't wait to follow your own dreams and end up full of regrets instead of memories. No matter how much life you've lived at this point, you don't really know how much is left. Once I was diagnosed, I realized that I didn't really have much of a bucket list of places I just had to visit anymore. And I certainly didn't want to jump out of an airplane or anything nutzoid like that. It's not like I've seen and done it all, but after 17 years of following my full-time RVing dreams all over this country, I can definitely say I've seen enough to look toward the end of my life with no regrets, at least as far as fulfilling my main dreams and the goals I valued.

As I look back over my life and sometimes start with the self recriminations, even when I get down and can't stand myself, a part of me always remembers that God loves me unconditionally with a depth and breadth that has always existed. Even when I judge everything in this world around me as being totally screwed up, I at least try to remember that *It is ALL Right and ALL is Well.*

And despite it all, I'm still willing to trade security for adventure. - Malia Lane

EPILOGUE

For my entire life, the hardest part of making my dreams come true was getting past my own limited beliefs about myself and my insecurities. As far as writing this book, was I capable and worthy enough to tackle something so important? There was so much to say about fear, but who was I to think I could effectively do that? And really, aren't there enough books in the world already?

I wondered how I could begin to teach others about being fearless or even fearing less when I was so filled with fear and doubts - despite all the evidence I've had to the contrary and the blessings I've been given and all the angels I've met?

Yet the calming answer that spoke from my soul was, "Do you think you're the only one with fear and doubts? Remember, you don't have to be perfectly fearless. If you or anyone else believed that perfection was required, it would cause you to give up - that is setting too high of a goal. Your experience shows how it's possible to feel fear and still be able to move forward. All you need to do is share that with others."

Nothing sticks better than having your own words shoved down your throat. It's not like you can deny that you once had those thoughts or looked at things from a more positive viewpoint instead of the negativity of gloom and doom. It was most interesting to see that my collection of fear and apprehensions about what might happen never happened and what negative things did happen weren't deal breakers as I had feared. I could have saved myself a lot of pain if I had concentrated more on the blessings instead of the challenges.

Since 2001 I have had an abundance of proof that miracles and angels accompany me every day, yet I was still afraid and insecure much of the time. I told myself constantly that if I just had more money and didn't have to worry about making a living every minute of every day, I wouldn't be so afraid and could just relax and enjoy my life. My more spiritually evolved secure self, knows this is total BS, but I still let fear associated with finances rule. Now I'm at a point where the length of my life cannot be bought at any price. And still I value the quality of my life more than the longevity and I am thankful I have at least a measure of control over that aspect.

An update on my first earth angel, Don: After he returned to Texas, he went back to his architect roots for a while and did a major remodeling job in Galveston. His health prevents him from still traveling now, but he's still as feisty as ever and living in his Airstream on some acreage at his daughter's home near Austin. We keep in touch regularly, and we look forward to meeting up "on the other side" again.

My advice for those in the beginning stages of following their dreams: strive to fear less along the way and keep a journal of your adventures, as these memories will be precious. More than that, there will be important lessons that will emerge that we don't comprehend at the time. Retrospect can be interesting, fascinating and enlightening, but unfortunately, only in retrospect.

From the book, Serenity:

> *I am convinced that as a child of God,*
> *I am called to risk...without risk there*
> *is no opportunity for personal growth.*

Could it be that you pretty much get in life what you are willing to pursue whole-heartedly, without reservation - not just what you sit back and hope and yearn for?

Just Fear Less, my friends — and trust more in the process. Take those baby steps toward your dreams and don't worry about being perfectly Fearless!

> *Feel the Fear but practice Faith*
> *and Trust Spirit to do the rest.*

ABOUT THE AUTHOR
Malia Miles Lane

Malia Lane is a native of New Orleans. She moved to Texas where she raised her daughters before pursuing her dream of traveling solo, full-time in an RV. She figured buying a house on wheels was her best bet to make her 'crazy' dream come true. She says, "I'm a homebody. I just like to change my yard out frequently. That's what I love the most about RVing - my home and all its comfy furniture and efficient kitchen is always with me. I don't have to worry about what I forgot to pack and I know my bathroom is always clean."

Following her dreams required facing many challenges along the way and a wide variety of fears head on. Her message to the world would be not to wait to follow your dream because none of us know what the future holds. She feels fortunate to have caught a glimpse of what she believes awaits her on the other side. She reminds us that being fearless is not required but fearing less is the only necessary goal. And that *It is ALL Right and All is Well.*

Malia's website and blog: www.MaliasMiles.com . There are literally thousands of pictures and more details on her adventures, so for those who want "the rest of the story," that's the site to check out.

58767440R00083

Made in the USA
Columbia, SC
24 May 2019